Descent to the Goddess

Marie-Louise von Franz, Honorary Patron

**Studies in Jungian Psychology
by Jungian Analysts**

Daryl Sharp, General Editor

Descent to the Goddess

A Way of Initiation for Women

Sylvia Brinton Perera

Canadian Cataloguing in Publication Data

Perera, Sylvia Brinton, 1932-
 Descent to the goddess

(Studies in Jungian psychology; 6)

Bibliography: p.
Includes index.

ISBN 0-919123-05-8

1. Women - Psychology. 2. Identity (Psychology).
3. Dreams. 4. Jung, C. G. (Carl Gustav), 1875-1961.
I. Title. II. Series.

HQ1206.P47   155.6′33   C81-094394-8

INNER CITY BOOKS
Box 1271, Station Q, Toronto, Canada M4T 2P4.

Honorary Patron: Marie-Louise von Franz.
Publisher and General Editor: Daryl Sharp.

INNER CITY BOOKS was founded in 1980 to promote the
understanding and practical application of the work of C. G.
Jung.

*Sylvia Brinton Perera is a Jungian Analyst practising in New
York City. She is a graduate of the C. G. Jung Training Center
in New York, and a member of its faculty.*

Cover: The goddess Inanna-Ishtar. Terracotta. Sumerian
Period (Louvre). Design by Jessie.
Index and Glossary by Daryl Sharp.

Set in Times.
Printed and bound in Canada by Webcom Limited.

CONTENTS

See last page for descriptions of other

Introduction

The return to the goddess, for renewal in a feminine source-ground and spirit, is a vitally important aspect of modern woman's quest for wholeness. We women who have succeeded in the world are usually "daughters of the father"—that is, well adapted to a masculine-oriented society—and have repudiated our own full feminine instincts and energy patterns, just as the culture has maimed or derogated most of them. We need to return to and redeem what the patriarchy has often seen only as a dangerous threat and called terrible mother, dragon, or witch.[1]

The patriarchal ego of both men and women, to earn its instinct-disciplining, striving, progressive, and heroic stance, has fled from the full-scale awe of the goddess. Or it has tried to slay her, or at least to dismember and thus depotentiate her. But it is towards her—and especially towards her culturally repressed aspects, those chthonic and chaotic, ineluctable depths—that the new individuating, yin-yang balanced ego must return to find its matrix and the embodied and flexible strength to be active and vulnerable, to stand its own ground and still to be empathetically related to others.

This return is often seen as part of the developmental pattern of women—what Erich Neumann calls a reconnection to the Self (the archetype of wholeness and regulating center of the personality) after the wrenching away from the mother by the patriarchal uroboros and the patriarchal marriage partner.[2] But Adrienne Rich speaks for many of us when she writes, "The woman I needed to call my mother was silenced before I was born."[3] Unfortunately, all too many modern women have not been nurtured by the mother in the first place. Instead, they have grown up in the difficult home of abstract, collective authority—"cut off at the ankles from earth," as one woman put it—full of superego shoulds and oughts. Or they have identified with the father and their patriarchal culture, thus alienating themselves from their own feminine ground and the personal mother, whom they have often seen as weak or irrelevant.[4] Such women have all the more necessity to meet the goddess in her primal reality.

This inner connection is an initiation essential for most

7

modern women in the Western world; without it we are not whole. The process requires both a sacrifice of our identity as spiritual daughters of the patriarchy and a descent into the spirit of the goddess, because so much of the power and passion of the feminine has been dormant in the underworld — in exile for five thousand years.

Tablet containing first half of poem, "The Descent of Inanna."
(Hilprect Collection, University of Jena)

I Descent and Return

The Myth of Inanna-Ishtar and Ereshkigal

There are many myths and tales about the descent of and to the goddess: for instance the Japanese Izanami, the Greek Kore-Persephone, Roman Psyche, and the fairytale heroines who go to Mother Hulda or Baba Yaga or the gingerbread house witch. The oldest known myth that states this motif was written on clay tablets in the third millenium B.C. (though it is probably much older, reaching into preliterate times). It is usually known as "The Descent of Inanna," the Sumerian queen of heaven and earth.[5] There are two later Akkadian versions based on this source, but with variations that we know as "Ishtar's Descent."[6]

In the Sumerian poem Inanna decides to go into the underworld; she "set her heart from highest heaven on earth's deepest ground,"[7] "abandoned heaven, abandoned earth—to the Netherworld she descended."[8] As a precaution, she instructs Ninshubur, her trusted female executive, to appeal to the father gods for help in securing her release if she does not return within three days.

At the first gate to the Netherworld, Inanna is stopped and asked to declare herself. The gatekeeper informs Ereshkigal, queen of the Great Below, that Inanna, "Queen of Heaven, of the place where the sun rises,"[9] asks for admission to the "land of no return" to witness the funeral of Gugalanna, husband of Ereshkigal. Ereshkigal becomes furious, and insists that the upper-world goddess be treated according to the laws and rites for anyone entering her kingdom—that she be brought "naked and bowed low."

The gatekeeper follows orders. He removes one piece of Inanna's magnificent regalia at each of the seven gates. "Crouched and stripped bare," as the Sumerians were laid in the grave, Inanna is judged by the seven judges. Ereshkigal kills her. Her corpse is hung on a peg, where it turns into a side of green, rotting meat. After three days, when Inanna fails to return, her assistant Ninshubur sets in motion her

9

instructions to rouse the people and gods with dirge drum and lamenting.

Ninshubur goes to Enlil, the highest god of sky and earth, and to Nanna, the moon god and Inanna's father. Both refuse to meddle in the exacting ways of the underworld. Finally Enki, the god of waters and wisdom, hears Ninshubur's plea and rescues Inanna, using two little mourners he creates from the dirt under his fingernail. They slip unnoticed into the Netherworld, carrying the food and water of life with which Enki provides them, and they secure Inanna's release by commiserating with Ereshkigal, who is now groaning—over the dead, or with her own birth pangs. She is so grateful for empathy that she finally hands over Inanna's corpse. Restored to life, Inanna is reminded that she will need to send a substitute to take her place. Demons to seize this scapegoat surround her as she returns through the seven gates and reclaims her vestments.

The last part of the myth involves the search for her substitute. Inanna does not hand over anyone who mourned for her. But finally she comes upon her primary consort, Dumuzi (later called Tammuz), who sits enjoying himself on his throne. Inanna looks on him with the same eyes of death Ereshkigal had set on her, and the demons seize him. Dumuzi flees with the help of Utu, who is the sun god and Inanna's brother. Utu transforms him into a snake to permit escape. In a related poem, Dumuzi dreams of his downfall. He goes to his sister, Geshtinanna, who helps him to interpret his dream and urges him to flee. When flight proves useless, she shelters him and finally offers to sacrifice herself in his stead. Inanna decrees that they shall divide the fate and spend half a year each in the underworld. The final poem ends with the words:

> Inanna placed Dumuzi in the hands of the eternal.
> Holy Ereshkigal! Sweet is your praise![10]

*

This myth and the goddesses Inanna, Ereshkigal, and Geshtinanna have moved and oriented me since I discovered the Kramer translations in 1973. I have found that by relating to this very early material—from an age when the Great Goddess was still vital—I have been able to reclaim some of my own relation to the archetypal feminine instinct and spirit patterns.

I cannot know precisely what these stories meant to the Sumerians, but they hold a cosmic pattern, one that is astronomical, seasonal, transformational, and psychological. And they have served as a projection screen from which I have tried to see a way of healing some of the psychological wounds in myself, in my women friends and colleagues, and in the unmothered women with whom I work in therapy. We all have grown up under the patriarchy and struggle with similar problems. The clinical material I shall use comes from dreams and experiences of my own, my friends, and my analysands.

Daughters of the Patriarchy

It is precisely the woman who has a poor relation to the mother, the one through whom the Self archetype first constellates, who tends to find her fulfillment through the father or the male beloved. She may be a woman who can find no relation to the Demeter-Kore myth because she "cannot believe," as one put it, that "any mother would be there to mourn or to receive" her again if she vanished into a crevasse. She may have an intense experience in the contrasexual sphere, but she lacks the ballast of a solid ego-Self connection. One patient expressed this early in her analysis almost as a manifesto:

> I insist on caring coming from a man. A female source enrages me. A male is in charge of the universe. Females are second best. I hate tunnels and Kali and my mother and this female body. A man is what I want.

The speaker was a young woman who had come into therapy because, although she was considered an excellent student, she was having difficulty writing her Ph.D. thesis.

The problem is that we who are badly wounded in our relation to the feminine usually have a fairly successful persona, a good public image. We have grown up as docile, often intellectual, daughters of the patriarchy, with what I call "animus-egos." We strive to uphold the virtues and aesthetic ideals which the patriarchal superego has presented to us. But we are filled with self-loathing and a deep sense of personal ugliness and failure when we can neither meet nor mitigate the superego's standards of perfection.

One woman with more than a decade of Jungian analysis

told me recently, "I have spent years trying to relativize something I never had—a real ego." And indeed she has only an animus-ego, not one of her own, with which to relate to the unconscious and the outer world. Her identity is based on persona adaptations to what her animus tells her should be, so she adapts to and rebels against the projections hooked onto her; thus she has almost no sense of her own personal core identity, her feminine value and standpoint. For what has been valued in the West in women has too often been defined only in relation to the masculine: the good, nurturant mother and wife; the sweet, docile, agreeable daughter; the gently supportive or bright, achieving partner. As many feminist writers have stated through the ages, this collective model (and the behavior it leads to) is inadequate for life; we mutilate, depotentiate, silence, and enrage ourselves trying to compress our souls into it, just as surely as our grandmothers deformed their fully breathing bodies with corsets for the sake of an ideal.[11]

We also feel unseen because there are no images alive to reflect our wholeness and variety. But where shall we look for symbols to suggest the full mystery and potency of the feminine and to provide images as models for personal life? The later Greek goddesses and Mary, Virgin Mother and Mediator, have not struck me to the core as have Inanna-Ereshkigal, Kali, and Isis.[12] An image for the goddess as Self needs to have a full-bodied coherence. So I have had to see the female Greek deities as partial aspects of one wholeness pattern and to look always for the darker powers hidden in their stories— the Gorgon aspect of Athena, the underworld Aphrodite-Urania, the Black Demeter, etc.

Even in the tales of Inanna and other early Sumerian, Semitic, and Egyptian writings there is evidence that the original potencies of the feminine have been "demoted." As Kramer tells us, the goddesses "that held top rank in the Sumerian pantheon were gradually forced down the ladder by male theologians" and "their powers turned over to male deities."[13] This permitted cerebral-intellectual-Apollonian, left brain consciousness, with its ethical and conceptual discriminations, to be born and to grow.[14]

It meant that the original creatress deity was differentiated —broken up into different aspects. In Sumer, the sea goddess

Nammu gave birth to various deities, and earth was carried off from heaven, just as "Ereshkigal was carried off into the *kur* [a word for Netherworld, desert, wilderness—a desolate, alien place] as its prize."[15] Already in ancient Sumer (and although the goddess of writing was female) by the time of written tales, an archetypal division and depotentiation of the goddess archetype had been made. The Great Goddess had been split in various ways, including into upper and lower world aspects. Thus there was a necessity to traverse both regions to restore a sense of creative wholeness and to comprehend the rhythmic interplay of life. Inanna, Queen of Heaven, was perhaps the first initiate described in writing to suffer this journey.

Four Perspectives on the Myth

Inanna's descent to and return from Ereshkigal can be seen from at least four perspectives. First, it serves as an image descriptive of the rhythmic order of nature: seasonal vegetation, the dwindling and replenishing of the storehouse,[16] the transformation of grain and grape by fermentation, and the alternations of the planet Inanna (our Venus). This planet stays in the sky as evening or morning star for 250 and 236 days respectively; then it seems to descend below the horizon as it disappears in front of or behind the sun for a period of time before it rises on the other side of night.

Secondly, it is a story of an initiation process into the mysteries. There is a gate into and out of the underworld later called Inanna-Ishtar's door. Through it others who made the journey to become conscious of the underworld were advised to pass.[17] Inanna's path and its stages may thus present a paradigm for the life-enhancing descent into the abyss of the dark goddess and out again. Inanna shows us the way, and she is the first to sacrifice herself for a deep feminine wisdom and for atonement. She descends, submits, and dies. This openness to being acted upon is the essence of the experience of the human soul faced with the transpersonal.[18] It is not based upon passivity, but upon an active willingness to receive.

The process of initiation in the esoteric and mystical traditions in the West involves exploring different modes of consciousness and rediscovering the experience of unity with nature and the cosmos that is inevitably lost through goal-directed development. This necessity—for those destined to it—forces us to go deep to reclaim modes of consciousness which are different from the intellectual, "secondary process" levels the West has so well refined. It forces us to the affect-laden, magic dimension and archaic depths that are embodied, ecstatic, and transformative; these depths are preverbal, often pre-image, capable of taking us over and shaking us to the core.

In those depths we are given a sense of the one cosmic power; there we are moved, and taught through the intensity of our affects that there is a living balance process. On those levels the conscious ego is overwhelmed by passion and numinous images. And, though shaken, even destroyed as we knew ourselves, we are recoalesced in a new pattern and spewed back into ordinary life. That journey is the goal of the initiation mysteries and of work on the astral plane in magic, even as it is the goal of therapeutic regression (for both men and women). The need for this journey fuels the current interest in the psychology of creativity and the early, pre-oedipal stages of human development and their pathologies.

Connecting to these levels of consciousness involves a sacrifice of the upper-world aspects of the Self to and for the sake of the dark, different, or altered-state aspects. It means sacrifice to and for the repressed, undifferentiated ground of being with the hope of gaining rebirth with a deeper, resonant awareness. And it means returning with those resonances, adding them to mental-cerebral, ordinary Western consciousness, in order to forge what Jean Gebser calls integral consciousness.[19] From this perspective the story of Inanna's descent is the revelation of an initiation ritual, and it is directly relevant to feminine experience today.

Consequently, the myth is also a description of a pattern of psychological health for the feminine, both in women and in men. It provides a model of the incarnation-ascension rhythm of the healthy soul, and also of a process to promote healing. "The soul comes 'from the stars' and returns to the stellar regions," writes Jung.[20] Inanna's descent, as we shall see, may be viewed as the incarnation of cosmic, uncontained powers into timebound, corrupting flesh, but it is also a descent for the purpose of retrieving values long repressed, and of uniting above and below into a new pattern.

I have often found myself oriented in deep analytic processes by this myth, for it shows, by analogy, how the conscious ideal of the personality—what we could call the ego-ideal, or the hypertrophic, superego-ridden animus-ego—when it has been wounded by being cut off from its roots by the devaluation of matter and the feminine, can approach the dark forces of earthly reality and the unconscious: slowly peeling away defenses and persona-identifications, in a controlled regression to those primary-process, beginning levels where the death of inadequate patterns and the birth of the authentic, validated, balanced ego awaits us. This myth shows us also how those dark, repressed levels may be raised, and how they may enter conscious life—through emotional upheavals and grief—to radically change conscious energy patterns.

Lastly, this tale may suggest some orientation in our own perilous age as the powers of the goddess return to Western culture. The return of Inanna from the underworld was at first demonic (even though it restored fruitfulness to the earth, which was barren when the goddess was absent), yet finally, as I read it, engendered a new model of equal and comradely relationship between woman and man (see chap. 9).

Our planet is passing through a phase—the return of the goddess—presaged at the beginning of the patriarchy in this myth. Its emphasis then was on the descent of the goddess, the loss to culture of her energies and symbols, and the subsequent retrieval of the powers symbolized in Ereshkigal. Our age can appreciate the full *circulatio,* for more and more of the feminine was repressed, and it has been too long in the underworld.

II Above and Below: Qualities of the Feminine

The Goddess Inanna

The goddess Inanna (her Semitic name is Ishtar) provides a many-faceted symbolic image, a wholeness pattern, of the feminine beyond the merely maternal. Other goddesses in Sumer were great sea and earth mothers. And while Inanna takes the double-axe symbol of the ancient goddesses into her cult, she combines earth and sky, matter and spirit, vessel and light, earthly bounty and heavenly guidance. She had perhaps originally to do with grain and the communal storehouse as vessel, the container of dates and grain and livestock. Among her oldest emblems were this storehouse and a looped cloth or bundle—perhaps of reeds as the closure to her storehouse— and the date god was one of her earliest divine bridegrooms.[21] She is thus, like Demeter and Ceriddwen, a numen of impersonal fertility.[22] In one song, she is said to pour forth grains and legumes from her womb.[23]

She is also, from the beginning, a goddess of the heavens, marked on ancient seals and vases as a star. As goddess of gentle rains and terrible storms and floods, and of the overcast sky (the clouds of which were called her breasts), she is called queen of heaven and said to be spouse of An, the ancient heaven god. She is also from very early times goddess of the radiant, erratic morning and evening star, awakening life and setting it to rest, ruling the borderlands, ushering in or out her brother the sun god and her father the moon god. She represents the liminal, intermediate regions, and energies that cannot be contained or made certain and secure. She is not the feminine as night, but rather she symbolizes consciousness of transition and borders, places of intersection and crossing over that imply creativity and change and all the joys and doubts that go with a human consciousness that is flexible, playful, never certain for long.

As evening star she holds court at the time of the new

16

moon to hear the gods' petitions and to be celebrated with music, feasting, and staged, bloody battles. She claimed the *me*, the ordering principles, potencies, talents and rites, of the civilized, upper world. And as judge, she holds court to "decree fate" and to "trample the disobedient," symbolizing the feeling capacity to evaluate, periodically and afresh, that goes with the sense of life as a changing process.

As queen of the land and its fertility, she bestows kingship on the mortal chosen to be shepherd of the people, and welcomes him to her bed and throne (made of a world tree which Gilgamesh cut down from her garden).[24] To her consort she gives throne, scepter, staff, crook, and crown, as well as the promise of good harvest and the joys of her bed.

But she is also goddess of war. Battle is "the dance of Inanna," and giving victory, she is "the quiver ready at hand, . . . the heart of the battle, . . . the arm of the warriors."[25] More passionate than Athena (with the energies of wild instinct which were later in Greece assigned to Artemis), she is described in one hymn as "all-devouring in . . . power . . . attacking like the attacking storm," having an "awesome face" and "angry heart,"[26] and she sings with abandoned delight of her own glory and prowess: "Heaven is mine, earth is mine,—I, a warrior am I. Is there a god who can vie with me?"[27] "The gods are sparrows—I am a falcon; the Anunnaki [the gods] trundle along—I am a splendid wild cow."[28] In one myth she is described as battling the dragon of *kur* and slaying it. Her companion animal is the lion, and seven of them pull her chariot. Sometimes, on ancient seals, she is accompanied by a scorpion.

Equally passionately, she is goddess of sexual love. She sings ecstatic songs of self-adornment and desire and of the delights of lovemaking. She calls to her beloved consort, her "honey-man" who "sweetens me ever,"[29] inviting him to her "holy lap" to savor her life-giving caresses and the sweetness of sex with her on the sacred marriage bed. More extraverted than Aphrodite, she craves and takes, desires and destroys, and then grieves and composes songs of grief. She does not as often arouse desire from within, but claims her need assertively and celebrates her body in song. *Her receptivity is active.* She calls out to have her body filled, singing praises to her vulva, and bidding Dumuzi come to her bed to "Plow my vulva, man of my heart."[30] She is thus goddess of courtesans, called harlot "hailing men from the alehouse" as she rises as evening star. And in heaven she is called bridesmaid and hierodule (high priestess and ritual prostitute) of the gods.

She is also healer, lifegiver, composer of songs—to which she is said to give birth, creative in all realms. And the behavior of the emotions is considered to be in her keeping:

> To pester, insult, deride, desecrate—and to venerate—is your domain, Inanna.
> Downheartedness, calamity, heartache—and joy and good cheer—is your domain, Inanna.
> Tremble, afright, terror—and dazzling and glory—is your domain, Inanna.... [31]

The many poems about her portray her as loving, jealous, grieving, joyful, timid, exhibitionistic, thieving, passionate, ambitious, generous, and so on; the whole range of affects is of the goddess.

Often Inanna is described as "daughter" of the gods, and "maid." And indeed, by the time the later hymns to her were written, she, like Athena, is often seen as "conditioned by bondedness to the father,"[32] although poems suggest a close, joyful, personal relationship to her own mother. Though she has two sons and the kings and people of Sumer are called her progeny, she is not motherly in our use of the term. Like the goddess Artemis, she is at the "border-*region* midway between motherhood and maidenhood *joie de vivre* and lust for murder, fecundity and animality."[33] She is a quintessential, positive puella, an eternally youthful, dynamic, fierce, sensuous, harlot-virgin (in Esther Harding's term, "one-in-herself"). She is never a settled and domestic wife nor mother under the patriarchy. She keeps her independence and magnetism as lover, young bride, and widow. And she is not a mother-lover, to sons. That role and concept seems to me to be an invention of the patriarchy and of times when women were depotentiated and lived their potential in projection on envied and beloved male offspring.[34]

And yet, in spite of her power as goddess of fertility, order, war, love, the heavens, healing, emotions, and song; in spite of having the titles Lady of Myriad Offices and Queen, Inanna is a wanderer. Like Ereshkigal, she was dispossessed by Enlil, the second generation sky god. Her roots lie deep in the prepatriarchal stratum, but from the perspective of the patriarchy, with Gilgamesh as its spokesman, Inanna-Ishtar is fickle and unreliable, and the certain cause of grief to her beloved consorts.[35] Thus Gilgamesh, who originally lent her his human strength to build the bed and throne of kingship, turns against her and derogates and insults the goddess of the land in order to claim her power. In one plaintive song Inanna laments to Enlil the loss of her house:

> Me the woman he has filled with dismay...
> Has filled me, the queen of heaven, with consternation...
> I, the woman who circles the land—tell me where is my house,
> Tell me where is the city in which I may live...
> I, who am your daughter... the hierodule, who am your brides-
>   maid—tell me where is my house...
> The bird has its nesting place, but I—my young are dispersed,
> The fish lies in calm waters, but I—my resting place exists not,
> The dog kneels at the threshold, but I—I have no threshold....[36]

The song may have been written to lament some calamity to her main temple in Erech. But beyond that, this is perhaps the oldest known and a very poignant statement of the condition of the goddess and woman as exile. Like the later Babylonian wives of Israel sent away from their homes by the patriarchy,[37] even the great pre-Babylonian goddess knows and sings of expulsion. In fact, the search for a home is one of the recurrent dream themes in the initial analytic work of modern women, daughters of the patriarchy.

Indeed, much of what Inanna symbolized for the Sumerians has since then been exiled. Most of the qualities held by the upper-world goddess have been desacralized in the West or taken over by masculine divinities, and/or they have been overly compressed or overly idealized by the patriarchal moral and aesthetic codes. Thus most of the Greek goddesses were swallowed up by their fathers; the Hebrew goddess was depotentiated. We are left with particularized or minimized goddesses. And most of the powers once held by the goddess have lost their connection to a woman's life: the embodied, playful, passionately erotic feminine; the powerful, independent, self-willed feminine; the ambitious, regal, many-sided feminine.

Women themselves have lived mainly in the personal realm, on the periphery of Western culture in narrowly circumscribed roles, often subordinating themselves to males, social position, children, etc., veiling their needs for power and passion,[38] living safely, secondary to the overburdened males on whom potency was projected and for whom it is culturally legitimate. What became collectively acceptable behavior for women lost its connection to the sacred as the full scale of the goddess was diminished. The patriarchal superego, originally necessary to inculcate ethical sensitivity, then strengthened by the institutional Christian Church to discipline the wild, tribal emotions of the medieval world, became increasingly hypertrophic.[39] Since the rise of Utilitarianism and Victorianism, it has so overconstricted and repressed life energies that they must now erupt, forcing, among other things, the return of the goddess into Western culture.

Constricted, the joy of the feminine has been denigrated as mere frivolity; her joyful lust demeaned as whorishness, or sentimentalized and maternalized; her vitality bound into duty and obedience. This devaluation produced ungrounded daughters of the patriarchy, their feminine strength and passion split off, their dreams and ideals in the unobtainable heavens, maintained grandly with a spirit false to the instinctual patterns symbolized by the queen of heaven and earth. It also produced frustrated furies. For as Inanna lives unconsciously in women under the patriarchy's repression, she is too often demonic. Actress June Havoc's description of the women of her family provides a portrait of the goddess' ebullient energies ground down and soured:

> All the women of [our] family...had a common strain of ambition and strength and bitter independence; they married early, divorced quickly, and in the end succumbed to alcohol or drugs or madness. They wanted total freedom and since they didn't know how to go about achieving it, they were hideously frustrated. Men were a convenience to them; they had an inability to enjoy love.[40]

On the other hand, lived consciously, the goddess Inanna in her role as suffering, exiled feminine provides an image of the deity who can, perhaps, carry the suffering and redemption of modern women. Closer to many of us than the Church's Christ, she suggests an archetypal pattern which can give meaning to women's quest,[41] one which may supplant the Christian myth for those unable to relate to a masculine God. Inanna's suffering, disrobing, humiliation, flagellation and death, the stations of her descent, her "crucifixion" on the underworld peg, and her resurrection, all prefigure Christ's passion and represent perhaps the first known archetypal image of the dying divinity whose sacrifice redeems the waste-land earth. Not for humankind's sins did Inanna sacrifice herself, but for earth's need for life and renewal. She is concerned more with life than with good and evil. Nonetheless her descent and return provide a model for our own psycho-logical-spiritual journeys.

And unlike Christ's story, where the destructive acts perpetrated on the savior were the product of mere human malice and fear—and thus capable of establishing a pattern of human revenge and scapegoating—in the Sumerian poem they are shown to have a transpersonal source. The goddess destroys, just as the goddess may redeem. And this leads us to a consideration of Ereshkigal, Inanna's dark "sister."

Ereshkigal, the Dark Goddess

The other major goddess of this myth is Ereshkigal, queen of the Netherworld and the dead. Her name means "Lady of the Great Place Below," but before being relegated to the *kur,* the alien place outside patriarchal consciousness, she was a grain goddess and lived above.[42] Thus she symbolizes the Great Round of nature, grain above and growing, and seed below and dying to sprout again. To matriarchal consciousness she represents the continuum in which different states are simply experienced as transformations of one energy. To the patriarchy death becomes a rape of life, a violence to be feared and controlled as much as possible with distance and moral order.

In a myth describing the events which led to the birth of the moon god, these two perspectives are set side by side. For in the upper world—as grain goddess—Ereshkigal was named Ninlil and called wife of Enlil, the second-generation sky god. Ninlil was repeatedly raped by her husband in various disguises.[43] On behalf of the young goddess the gods punished Enlil for the violence he perpetrated on her: they sent him to the underworld. Out of love for her consort, Ninlil followed

him down and became known as Ereshkigal. Enlil continued
to appear as the ruling sky god in heaven, but he may have
had an underworld form. Just as Zeus of the underworld was
named Hades,[44] so Enlil may well be the Gugalanna of the
Descent myth, the Great Bull of Heaven, husband of Ereshkigal, who has been killed.

From the perspective of the patriarchy, the rape of the
goddess establishes masculine rule over conscious cultural life
(and perhaps over agriculture) and relegates feminine power
and fertility to the underworld. Thus when the god An seized
heaven and Enlil carried off the earth, and consciousness had
space to grow, then "Ereshkigal was seized by the Great
Below as a prize."[45] But from the perspective of magic-matriarchal consciousness, the goddess is not a prize to be carried
out of life; nor is death a rape and a destruction of life, but
rather a transformation to which, like the grain to the reaper,
the goddess willingly surrenders and over which process she
rules.[46]

The poem describing Inanna's descent tells us that the first
of the rapes of Ninlil-Ereshkigal produced Nanna-Sin, the
moon god, who was born in the underworld and rises to light
the darkness and to measure time with his growing and wan-
ing cycles. Nanna-Sin, in fact, is Inanna's father (and father of
the sun god as well). Thus his mother, Ninlil-Ereshkigal, is
Inanna's grandmother in the geneology—an aspect of the
boundless, primal feminine which was raped, cut down, and
still bore fruit. Ereshkigal became a symbol of dread death to
the patriarchy, and was banished into the underworld. Nonetheless, the body of the poem recalls her archaic potency, and
the last line teaches the sweetness of coming to know her as
symbol of the Great Round.[47]

Qualities of Ereshkigal

Paradox

The fruits of the other rapes were said to have been monsters.
The Great Round produces a chaotic panoply which is monstrous to the patriarchal, heroic world view with its emphasis
on rational order and control. Ereshkigal defies differentiated
consciousness. She is paradoxical: both the vessel and the

stake. She is the root of all, where energy is inert and consciousness coiled asleep. She is the place where potential life lies motionless—but in the pangs of birth; beneath all language and its distinction, yet judging and acting. She is the energy banishing itself into the underworld, too awesome to behold—like primal childhood experiences and the darkness of the moon, places of oblivion that are the perilous ground on which daylight consciousness treads, the primal matrix. And she holds the wisdom of that isolation and bitterness. She is receiver of all, yet adversary and death-dealing inevitable victor. The myth shows her susceptible to initiatives from above, though she rules the Land of No Return, the realm of all that goes below the horizon of consciousness.

Her rape suggests analogies with the story of Persephone, but her image shows the earlier, paradoxical potency in raw form, and there is much of the Gorgon and of the Black Demeter about her: in her power and terror, the leeches on her head, her terrible life-freezing eyes, and her intimate connection to nonbeing and to fate. She holds and embodies the rules of the Netherworld as she sits with her seven judges[48] to receive whomever comes to her through the seven gates of her lapis lazuli house. In other myths her consort is Ninazu (lord of healing) or Nergal (god of plague, war, and death).[49]

Primal Affect

In the Descent poem Ereshkigal is described first as enraged due to Inanna's invasion of her realm; second, as actively destructive; third, as suffering; and finally as grateful and generous. In anger her face turns yellow, her lips black,[50] and she smites her thigh and bites herself.[51] She is concerned that Inanna will raise the dead, her own servants, and thus deprive her of bread and beer, and make her eat dust and water like the dead themselves.[52] Here there is a quality of primal rage about her. She is full of fury, greed, the fear of loss, and even of self-spite. She symbolizes raw instinctuality split off from consciousness—need and aggression in the underworld. And she sends her gatekeeper to deal with the intruder, a male to defend her.

These images suggest that chaotic defensive furies, such as rage, greed, and even the unleashing of the animus, are inevitable aspects of the archetypal underworld. They are the ways the unconscious reacts to unwelcome visitation. We see them when a complex is probed, for the unconscious has its own powerful defenses. They are part of the Great Goddess, the myth says; we feel these compulsive, unconscious energies working to overpower the ego. When the conscious personality is asked to confront such affects, it blocks, feels embarrassed, fears being shattered by superior strength, often retreats into anxiety or detachment, suspended out of life. It is at such points that the energies need to be reverenced, seen as aspects of the goddess which can be served and allowed consciously to enter life.

Energy

From the perspective of what happens to Inanna in the under-world we can see that the forces which Ereshkigal symbolizes are those connected not only to active destruction but also to transformation, via those slow, cell-by-cell organic processes, like decay and gestation, which work upon the passive, stuck recipient even invasively and against his or her own will. Such impersonal forces devour and destroy, incubate and bring to birth, with an implacable pitilessness. (Even pregnancy can be felt this way.) Here they act upon Inanna and reduce her to the primal state of inert animal matter itself—but matter that undergoes change, in passive submission to the given. It rots. Psychologically, Ereshkigal's force is often felt as negative— from the perspective of active, abstract, patriarchal, Logos consciousness. Then these forces bring about a hopeless, empty, shattering, numb, barren void or chaos.

Ereshkigal's domain, when we are in it, seems unbounded, irrational, primordial, and totally uncaring, even destructive of the individual. It contains an energy we begin to know through the study of black holes and the disintegration of elements, as well as through the processes of fermentation, cancer, decay, and lower brain activities that regulate peristal-sis, menstruation, pregnancy, and other forms of bodily life to which we must submit. It is the destructive-transformative side of the cosmic will. Ereshkigal is like Kali, who through time and suffering "pitilessly grinds down ... all distinctions ... in her indiscriminating fires"[53]—and yet heaves forth new life. She symbolizes the abyss that is the source and the end, the ground of all being.

Matter

Ereshkigal's energies are also those related to seeming stasis and the coalesced, unitive solidity of matter as a cosmic principle. They are the elementary, retaining, conserving, grounding forces closely related to the *muladhara* chakra, its instincts for survival and its fears for basic constancy and security.[54] Here energy "rests sleeping . . . static . . . in solid matter" as inertia,[55] the slowest vibrations of cosmic energy.

Such seeming stasis suggests the potential of cleansing immersion in the darkness of the unknown. But it also suggests a dissolution and slowness requiring great patience of those who enter. Ereshkigal's realm represents the one certainty of life—that we all die. Yet because of this very certainty, she is a manifestation of the most unknown and other, where active life's consciousness lies dormant. We are barely conscious when there is so little movement to stir our senses. We are reduced to the dark side of intuition, *muladhara*'s sense of smell, orienting us to the infinite and immortal potentials inherent in the passively received yet embodied and passing moment. Here there is both inertia and an elemental healing source. It is the place of survival and earth and rock solid beginnings. It is the place of the Self *in status nascendi*—the jewel hidden in matter—and also of the end as the return of activity into repose and death.

Natural Lawfulness

Ereshkigal's vizier is named Namtar, "fate." Her realm has its own lawfulness before which the sky gods of Sumer bow. It is the "law of the Great Below," the law of reality—things as they are—the natural law which is pre-ethical, often fearsome, always preceding the superego judgments of the patriarchy and often of what we would wish.

A woman who came into therapy in middle age, having lived with a competent and active animus-ego until her children left home, had severe colitis as a physical symptom. She wrote about her "return to the beginning below all the artifices and controls":

I grew up under what I now see is a false law—there is another. The true law is swallowing and breathing and shitting, all the processes of the body. There is no right or wrong, there is just what is. There is neither good nor bad, just what is necessary. It is a divine order I find by discovering it in my own body; not an imposed order, but an allowing. The balances of power keep changing, but they form of themselves if I can wait. But it's a balance with tension, not a dead balance. There's even an order in this chaotic analytic process, in my angers, even in the depression. A different kind of law and time and suffering.

This woman had been toilet trained in the first week of her life through the constant use of suppositories. She said, as she terminated therapy, "I see it's been a process from colitis to being an established shit-maker." Her initiation into the dark goddess and the Tantric anal-*muladhara* level was profound and taught me a great deal.

Analytic Experience of Ereshkigal

This basic yin ground, background, substratum, is a constant to which many daughters of the negative father[56] have little or no connection. Sometimes moments of terror evoke it negatively—as when a woman patient with pneumonia felt her chest fill up with earth, or when another in fear withdrew her soul so deeply into herself that she felt she was only a desolate stone, untouchable. Work on the images returned a sense of the potential embodied life hidden in the static, paralyzed state. Behind congealment for the first woman patient was the earth's warmth and a slow patience to turn towards her physical body in order to heal herself. Beyond the stone, when the second woman could look, was the sacred, timeless, fragile life of the deserts she loved and of pueblo culture that endures and values nature and even stones.

Unreverenced, Ereshkigal's forces are felt as depression[57] and an abysmal agony of helplessness and futility—unacceptable desire and transformative-destructive energy, unacceptable autonomy (the need for separateness and self-assertion) split off, turned in, and devouring the individual's sense of willed potency and value. A woman suffering Ereshkigal has unknowingly put her negative animus superego first and been overpowered. She is split off from her primal affects, has lost consciousness of them. Yet she falls easily into the underworld as into a vortex, or she follows a beloved man with psychopathic or psychotic tendencies, who can lead her into the depths. Or she seeks the underworld compulsively, hides from life, often addicted to various modes of dulling the pains of the flow of change which are too much for her fragmented capacity. Or else she may unconsciously identify with what the culture rejects as ineffective and inferior, forcing her to introvert through a negative sense of uniqueness.[58]

In identity with Ereshkigal, a woman can feel stuck in a timeless stasis, unable to budge, feeling the bleak despair and the emptiness of one raped by the animus.[59] She may be in identity with the goddess as the great maw, receiving back all life, feeling starved and greedy. Often she suffers somatic symptoms, disturbances related to abdominal organs, to digestion, or to cellular disintegrative processes.

It gives great solace to know which altar to approach when confronted with such states. But Ereshkigal does not want to be worshipped in the usual ways. Like the elementary, chthonic gods, to whom sacrifices were holocausted,[60] she demands death, complete destruction of differentiations and the felt sense of individuality, and total transformation. She demands a terrible empathy, one that surrenders, waits upon, and groans with her. On the archaic-magic level of consciousness her victims go gracefully, taken back into the maw. (And the Sumerians felt that direct attention and offerings stayed the hand of the most malevolent deities.)[61] But for us to serve and revere that power in its impersonal rhythms and destruction seems as monstrous as do her children. Thus we often deny or rage or armor and distance ourselves, in defense against the sense of helpless surrender to her impersonal and instinctual forces, seeking to dull the heroic ego's humiliation at being brought so low that we must confront our primal smallness in the cosmos. Yet only an act of conscious, willing surrender can turn that poisonous side of the dark goddess into life. The death of the active, differentiated, beautiful queen of heaven and the action of Enki's mourners in this story balance and fill Ereshkigal's seeming void.

Dream images of the abysmal goddess are not infrequent during phases of analysis when the conscious ego-ideal is to undergo mortification and to be radically transformed. One woman professor's nightmare was of a black planet approaching her at the hour she was to teach, spewing vapors that made her scholarly mind go blank. She felt "completely destroyed, as if there is no me left." An elegant, competent businesswoman was confronted in a dream with the image of "a fat, ugly creature, like a termite queen, slowly writhing in waves of birth or defecation." She was appalled to see something "so hideous and bestial." A third, a woman beginning to come to terms with her considerable intellectual and emotional capacities, who had previously identified herself as a wild eccentric child, dreamt:

> I am on a subway platform, trying to scrape up a package of hamburger meat that has fallen and spilled. Nearby looms a giant, black-robed, cold, sadistic woman who watches. She is like a queen cobra. She has the amoral face of darkness. She can do anything; she's not interested in life or being nice. She's objective, efficient, of this solid earth and as ruthless as it takes.

This dream presaged a depression in which her grandiose ego-ideal was ground down to prime meat, and she was forced to accept the positive shadow's previously feared, calm strength. She slowly undertook a new career and walked out of an unsatisfactory personal relationship. Later she dreamt that the dark woman had moved into her housekeeper's room, replacing a nice, homey, ineffective woman.

This underworld aspect of the feminine we meet often enough in analysis when animus-identified puella women descend into what the idealistic animus has branded evil or sick or ugly and loathsome. The regression or introversion is often so slow and deep that it may turn into a profound, deathlike depression, which may be very frightening if there is no orientation to its archetypal meanings and pattern. One previously active woman described this in her journal as:

> a slow decaying of all the shoulds, a dying of the encasements of my life that has felt like rotting. I have had to accept that slowness and the destruction of what I thought was me. There is always the fear that once I sacrifice the old, social, competent me, I will be dead. Yet in this depressed place, where I have felt inertia in the embrace of uttermost matter, like cement holding me, there has been an unbinding

of energy. It's been so deep I lose my sense of time—only know that my nails have grown and need cutting again. It's coming at everything slow and from below—not human and warm, but detached. Below ideas of mean or not mean.

Another said:

> I've been so low—it's been nauseous, like green meat. I've never let myself be so passive and full of the uglies, but I'm not even abashed anymore. It's a coming to know that I don't care, and so what. It seems so cold, but it has a strength that can receive and accept anything, even pain. So now I can feel at home in the universe. It balances some place I've been scared of all my life in my mother's fierceness and my fear and hate to touch a man's penis. I had to heal me there before I could relate without being blasted or going unconscious.

When we are reduced to the depths of numb pain and depression, to timelessness, preverbal chaos and emotionality—all that we call awful or infantile and associate with the archaic dimensions of consciousness—we can know that the goddess we must serve and revere is Ereshkigal. Contact with her grounds a woman. It coagulates feminine potency to confront the patriarchy and the masculine as an equal.

Ereshkigal's Rejection by the Patriarchy

Patriarchal consciousness has split off this goddess, raped her and relegated her to the underworld. We are enjoined against looking too closely at the awesome, destructive side of the nature goddess.[62] She has been carried out of our consciousness, and she abides in the depths of the unconscious. In her terrible form Ereshkigal never comes up. When the gods give a feast, they ask her to send someone to get her food.[63] Yet she is not antagonistic to the masculine. She is surrounded by male judges, her consorts and servants are male, she gives birth to sons. And she is easily turned from fury at Nergal, who was rude to her emissary. When he recognizes that "it was but love you wanted of me from months ago to now," she offers him marriage and rule over the Netherworld, which he accepts.[64]

Contrary to much that has been written, this myth suggests that the consciousness of the deep layers of the psyche is not an adversary of heroic, patriarchal consciousness—the sky gods. The forces and modalities of the Great Round do not wish to rule, or even to resist, hierarchical, progress-oriented, Logos modes. They do require reverence and respect, however. Ereshkigal rages when she is not met with respect. She is proud, but she does not mount an offensive, nor does she transgress her own boundaries. She simply demands recognition as an equal power, one as valid and important as the Great Above—as Nergal finally realized when he confronted her.

Rather, it is the defensive fear inherent in hierarchical, heroic consciousness that turns from the flow of change and its own split-off "infantile" impulses. Projecting these onto the mother, it sees her as enemy[65] and refuses to recognize her own kind of wisdom, which is as necessary to life as its own. It turns from its own source, for Ereshkigal is mother of the night's moon as well as of monsters, and she is grandmother of sun and star. From her womb issue the heavenly lights and the creatures of plague and death. She is the source of consciousness brought by the sky's patterning lights and by mortal fears and pains.

Closer to psychic reality than the view of hierarchical, patriarchal consciousness which derogates Ereshkigal, is the Tantric view that sees each chakra containing its own form of awareness, each providing a distinct perspective, all of which are to be welcomed as facets of a cosmic consciousness vibrating harmoniously together in the ideally awakened individual. But we are only creeping towards the realization of such a capacity for authentic, multivalent consciousness.[66]

The Objectivity of the Eyes of Death

There is affect and energy and lawfulness in Ereshkigal. There are also her eyes of death. For Inanna is killed and turned into meat by Ereshkigal in an action described in the poem with chilling awe:

> The holy Ereshkigal seated herself upon her throne...
> She fastened her eyes upon her [Inanna], the eyes of death,
> Spoke the word against her, the word of wrath,
> Uttered the cry against her, the cry of guilt,
> Struck her, turned her into a corpse.
> The corpse was hung from a nail.[67]

Sometimes in Sumerian poetry the expression "eyes of life" is used to suggest seeing that is full of love and gives vitality. The focus on describing the power of the eye recalls early images of the Eye Goddess, and the goddess as eye in Egypt, and of the vital importance of the mother's eyes to the nursing infant. When children first begin to draw faces the only features they include are those that see. In Sumerian and Babylonian sculpture, the eyes of gods and worshippers are enlarged and made into almost hypnotic, staring disks to convey their hieratic potency as seat of the soul.

Here in the poem, Ereshkigal's eyes combine with word, affect, the judgment of conscience, and the act of murder. They are the eyes of death, pitiless, not personally caring. To humans who are paralyzed with fear and lose sense of process and paradox, they can be the hateful glare that freezes life, like a mother's hate-envy that blights her child and makes an end of all beginnings—raw sadism and rage in its archetypal form. Or the eyes of depression, to which "all looks dead." They can be the eyes that transfix life, the projection of our human fear or rage, seizing a moment or an image and making it concrete and static. Such eyes bring psychosis; we see them in individuals suffering psychotic states, where the capacity to see through the tightly held fragment to the life process and spirit, in which the static frame inheres as a partial fact, is lost.

They can thus be the eyes that lose a sense of the greater whole. Or they can suggest a capacity to be objective, an unrelatedness to the other that is life- and self-affirmation at its basic demonic level—not what we like to think is feminine in our culture. And Jung, writing on the *muladhara* chakra, reminds us of the value of the negative aspect of the Self. There is an "aspect of hatred ... [which] one would describe in Western philosophical terms as an urge or instinct toward individuation,"[68] for its function is to destroy *participation mystique* by separating and setting apart an individual who had previously merged, identical with loved ones.

In the poem, Inanna, unveiled, sees her own mysterious depth, Ereshkigal, who glares back at her. She has an immediate, full experience of her underworld self. That naked moment is like the fifth scene in the Villa of Mysteries where the faun, looking into a mirror bowl, sees reflected back a mask of terrible Dionysus as lord of the underworld. It is the moment of self-confrontation for the goddess of active life and love.[69]

A woman dreamt: "I am handed the poison of the world. It is labelled 'uncaring.'" She had been struggling with what she thought was her lover's coldness. The dream image showed her, instead, that it was, and is, nature's coldness. And she herself—in identity with the victim who seeks subservient affiliations and merging through placation of her partner—must drink to find her communion with the goddess.

Archetypally, these eyes of death are implacable and profound, seeing an immediate is-ness that finds pretense, ideals, even individuality and relatedness, irrelevant. They also hold and enable the mystery of a radically different, precultural mode of perception. Like the eyes in the skulls around the house of the Russian nature goddess and witch, Baba-Yaga,[70] they perceive with an objectivity like that of nature itself and our dreams, boring into the soul to find the naked truth, to see reality beneath all its myriad forms and the illusions and defenses it displays.

Western science once aspired to such vision. But we humans do not have such objective eyes. We can see only limited and relative, indeterminate truths. We and our subjectivity are part of the reality we seek to see. Before the vision of Ereshkigal, however, objective reality is unmasked. It is nothing—"*Neti, neti*," as the Sanskrit says—and yet everything, the place of paradox behind the veil of the Great Goddess and the temple of wisdom. These eyes see from and embody the starkness of the abyss that takes all back, reduces the dancing, playing maya of the goddess to inert matter and stops life on earth.

These eyes obviate the patterns and ideals of habitual and collective rational consciousness—the way we see in linguistic confines, "trapped within conceptual spaces"[71] that form the world of differentiated appearances. They pierce through and get down to the substance of preverbal reality itself. They see, also, through collective standards that are false to life as it is. Thus they destroy identification with animus ideals. They make possible a perception of reality without the distortions and preconceptions of superego. This means seeing, not what might be good or bad, but what exists before judgment, which is always messy and full of affect and of the preverbal percepts of the near senses (touch, smell, taste). This implies not caring first and foremost about relatedness to an outer other, nor to a collective gestalt or imperative. Seeing this way—which is initially so frightening because it cannot be validated by the collective—can provide what Logos consciousness fears as mere chaos, with the possibilities of a totally fresh perception, a new pattern, a creative perspective, a never ending exploration.

Such seeing is radical and dangerously innovative, but not necessarily evil unless unbalanced and therefore static and partial. It feels monstrous and ugly and even petrifying to the non-initiate. For it shears us of our defenses and entails a sacrifice of easy collective understandings and of the hopes and expectations of looking good and safely belonging. It is crude, chaotic, surprising, giving a view of the ground below ethics and aesthetics and the opposites themselves. It is the instinctual eye—an eye of the spirit in nature. This is the vision that Ereshkigal and Kali and the Gorgon bring to the initiate. It is the meaning of the vision of the terrible guardian head at Siva's temples.[72] It is awful, and yet bestows a refined perception of reality to those who can bear it. This is the wisdom of the dark feminine that Psyche could not yet sustain—the knowledge she was to bring to Aphrodite, the Greek Inanna, to make her beautiful and eternal. Psyche saw it briefly and fell unconscious, for that age was not ready for such knowledge. Now we need to know this vision, for we are already working with its subtle energies in astro- and atomic physics.

Psychologically, this mode of seeing, this knowledge, implies that destruction and transformation into something even radically new are part of the cycle of reality.[73] As one woman put it:

> I see that you can't do anything without hurting someone, some sacrifice, some pain or betrayal—at least much of the time. That everything ends and begins somewhere else. Innocence is impossible.

Such knowledge is hard to endure. We try to pretty it up, cover, avoid. But knowing this basic reality permits a woman to give up trying to be agreeable to parental and animus imperatives and ideals. It is like hitting rock bottom, from where they are irrelevant. It relativizes all principles, and opens a woman to the paradoxes involved in living with the Self.

One woman forced to awareness of this vision dreamt of a beautiful lady with tiny skulls in her pupils, and through those eyes the dreamer saw into a vast night sky. Another woman had a vision of her dead grandmother with her eyes fallen into her head. She wrote, "Such eyes include everything. They see across to the ground of being and they can stand such objectivity. They mean pain is inevitable. I can't hide."

As an analyst I stand by that vision when I speak my own truth, saying, "That's how I feel now, that's what I see." It is objective and my moment's valid discrimination. But like a probe, it may hurt the one seen. And it may separate me from another. But when I lose connection to the solidity of that seeming coldness, or try to stave it off as the good mother or daughter, then my ego becomes ungrounded and the coldness falls into the unconscious and comes at me or the other from the animus. And when a woman in therapy projects that stony, *muladhara* vision onto me, and I am afraid to be seen that cold and to value it as transpersonal, feminine objectivity in which I share and which I value as self-protection, then I lose it and can be petrified, go unconscious with fear; I feel it coming at me out of the negative transference, and I want to plug up the other's rage.

This cool, objective eye is one basis—perhaps the left brain aspect—of feminine evaluation. It does not get deceived by responsible performance or willed achievement, but finds the ineluctable facts in process, the panoply of emotional vectors that give each moment life, and that pass as others crowd into the present, leaving the individual at the mercy of time and processes over which one has little control, but in which one may find a grounding if one can reverence change itself and find one's own way to move with it. Such vision is transpersonal and a power that can protect—so Athena, *gorgopis* (bright-eyed) and owl-eyed, wore the Gorgon's eyes on her shield; so Inanna later embodied the "eyes of death."

III   Suffering and Standing Separate

Suffering—Unconscious and Conscious

The seemingly cold yin of Ereshkigal's vision is intimately related, in the myth, to the suffering yin. Inanna hangs impaled, and Ereshkigal lies naked and groaning in misery of death or labor. She is described:

> The birth-giving mother, because of her children,
> Ereshkigal lies there ill, [perhaps in labor]
> Over her holy body no cloth is spread,
> Her holy chest like a *shagan* vessel is not [veiled][74]
> [her talons, like a copper rake (?) upon her[75]]
> Her hair like leeches she wears upon her head.[76]

Suffering is also a major part of the underworld feminine. It may be unconscious until the advent of the goddess of light awakens it to awareness, stirs the silent numbness to pain. On the magic level of consciousness, it is numbly endured.[77] There is no awareness of suffering.

But suffering *is* part of the feminine. We forget that until this century childbirth was often attended by death: so Aztec women who died in childbirth were equated with warriors who died in battle; so Anne Bradstreet wrote a poem bidding farewell to her husband and little ones when she went into labor with another child;[78] so Cotton Mather and his contemporaries saw that

> the Difficulties both of *Subjection* and of *Childbearing*, which the *Female Sex* is doom'd unto, ha's been turned into a *Blessing*, ... God Sanctifies the *Chains*, the *Pains*, the *Deaths* which they meet withal; ... [as] a further Occasion of Serious Devotion in them.[79]

Woman's life has been the reality of constantly recurring childbirths, attended by real deaths—a natural cycle that kept most of her life focussed on the harsh malevolence of reality, on a sense of living at the brink of the abyss. So women's creativity has gone into actual births and the arts and sustenance of the household—all subject to wear and destruction, to devouring—and not much appreciated in the wider cultural context; though they are the basic civilizing force of any culture, immediate, personal, made in the small interstices of the process of sustaining survival. It is no wonder, in this context, that Jewish men thank God they were not created female. But wounding for a woman is not necessarily pathology. It is part of the cycle of menses and birth and daily blood life.

Ereshkigal is caught in and embodies an ordained process: "that all life death doth end," that birth and death are intimates in the history of women, that change and pain are inevitable. She suffers in isolation, in patient submission, enduring. She reminds us that many of the great goddesses suffer, are wounded by separation from child or mother or lover. They do not avoid suffering, but face into it, and express its reality. Some, like Parvati, Shiva's intended, undertake suffering to elicit the beloved's attention and to restore life's balance. Some get stuck or impaled. For suffering can lead to terrible passivity, a negative inertia (like the Greek Perithous who got stuck in Hades). And in Ereshkigal's realm there is a standstill where all is miasmic and inhuman and inchoate. Inanna is impaled, Ereshkigal groans. There is no hope, no effective, yang answer, no way out by work or will. This is the other side of the coldness of the dark goddess.

Yet here suffering is a primal way. It is a sacrifice of activity which can lead even to rebirth and illumination when it is accepted as a way to let be. It suggests presence at its darkest level—a sense of loss of all, even the capacity for action, a loss so deep nothing matters, "pitched past pitch of grief."[80] It is the place of the powerlessness of chaotic and numb or unchanneled affect, the lonely grief-rage of powerlessness and unassuaged loss and longing, a hellish place where all we know to do is useless (thus there is no known way out of the despair). We can only endure, barely conscious, barely surviving the pain and powerlessness, suspended out of life, stuck, until and if, some act of grace with some new wisdom arrives. Such raw, impersonal, though potentially initiating miseries are Ereshkigal's domain.

Ereshkigal's Peg—Fixes and Incarnates

From this perspective Ereshkigal's peg can be felt as terrible and frightening, like one of the poles on which heads were hung around the Hindu and Celtic otherworld castles. One woman verbalized this misery: "There's pain because I was abandoned by my mother—like a spike in my heart. And all my life dead." It is the abysmal bereftness of the child of the death mother—a life of mortification. Another, speaking of her sense of deprivation as she began in analysis to reexperience it, said, "It's like a flayed phallus, an image of desire in hell, so raw it cannot even be touched to receive, so it is an empty craving." Her needs were split off (she was orphaned at two and sent to an institution), and they felt so acute and unobtainable in the human realm that they seemed only ugly and terrible. A third woman imaged in a dream her uncle's phallus as a pole on which she was suspended. She remembered his frightening physical advances and rages, but she had idealized him and was afraid to give up her own desirousness of men who resembled him, "because that feels like home." This cruel human sadism is like Ereshkigal's pole. It stops conscious human life. And often we find ourselves getting sick or "going crazy," rather than facing the reality of such pain.

But there is another side to the image of the stake. Unlike the scene in the later Egyptian myth where Isis fertilizes herself with Osiris's member when he is dead, here the dead partner is female. The Great Goddess is lifeless and penetrated while she is passive, empty of life, reduced to meat. There is no motion, no obvious quickening. There is only the placement of the body on the peg. With a terrible fixing, Inanna is nailed down. The potential of her "myriad offices" and capacities is grounded; and this actualization seems to be part of what fertilizes a new spirit within her, just as limitation can evoke creativity.

One woman expressed her experience of the painful side of this *fixatio:*

> It's as if my messy house is my cross. I'm utterly fixed—out of the fantasy of home and great life and being an important person. Just hanging there, and the old labels don't apply. I've lost all control of the way things used to be, and the pulling myself up by the bootstraps, and the shoulds. I stick to tiny details that nail me down. They are supports to get me through a pain that's not even dramatic and desperate, but just numb. There is no meaning, no comfort. I can only wait and wait. And it's not even waiting for rescue in the old way.

This 48-year-old woman had spent much of her life hoping to be recognized, hoping finally to be mothered, hoping to be acclaimed by a knight on a white charger who would redeem her passivity. Through analysis the quality of the inertia changed. She felt she could sacrifice her habitual dramas, her frantic, unconscious activity, and withdraw into the small details of her everyday life. She identified the humiliation she felt as akin to Christ's crucifixion, for she knew no way to have the cup taken from her, and she did not yet know the story of Inanna, nor feel connected to the feminine. After many months of focus on the incarnated facts of existence, she began to see that what she had sought was present within them when she was able to see from a new perspective. She began to do sensory awareness work, to honor her body with clothes that had color and texture. She found her feelings opening up in the transference relationship with her therapist. She began to value her incarnated and feeling life, and she could finally look back on her depression as a gift bringing her a new sense of her existence.

Another aspect of the incarnation potential in the stake was articulated by a woman who spoke about a newly awakened sense of the reality of her body:

> A woman is nailed to the cross when she begins to menstruate. That's why I hated it, pretended it was nothing. Then, with the energy of a bull, a woman has to take in that cross, allow it to pierce her and let herself be swung between its two horns. It's the order of nature for a woman, and a different kind of cross from the Christian, for we have to swing between the prongs through time. I always considered it dirty and the moodiness and pain of my period a real sacrifice, but I can see now— through my daughter's experience—that the energy there is the equal of phallic energy, only there are two prongs, making one bowl.

In spite of her conscious disgust for menstruation, this woman had an instinctive sense of the "bull of the mother," and her statement recalls the great horned altar at Crete and the horned moon god as lord of women.[81]

There is a possible connection between this sense of the horned god and the Gugalanna of the myth (see chap. 5). He is "killed" or actively deprived of his menstrual effect when a woman becomes pregnant. There may be a suggestion, from this perspective, that the Descent myth has reverberations concerning a central mystery of feminine experience, pregnancy.

There are several cultures in which a woman in labor is tied to or holds a tree for birthing. (Buddha's mother is one example, and some Amazon tribes practice the custom of tying the laboring mother off the ground, so she hangs until the child appears.) Certainly submission to the mystery of bodily experience is one way in which a woman, even the goddess, is nailed down into incarnated existence—nailed into reality to find her own firm stance.

This sense of the pole suggests an aspect of the impersonal feminine yang energy. It makes firm, nails down into material reality, embodies, and grounds spirit in matter and the moment. It is thus supportive, a peg to hang onto through life's flux. Also the stake is like a phallus or dildo of the dark goddess, or the member of Gugalanna her husband, who was killed. There are analogies to the cold phallus of the devil—lord of the underworld and consort of Diana—as the Western witch cult members felt it. For them this phallus joined them into one community through shared ritual experience of the impregnating spirit of nature.

Ereshkigal's Peg as Feminine Power to Stand Separate

The stake provides an opening penetration that is the instrument of the goddess' initiation, like the impersonal phallus of any man at the temples of Inanna-Ishtar. That rite Esther Harding saw as freeing the energies of sexual intercourse to the goddess.[82] Because the receptive yin is by nature empty, there is a danger that women feeling their own emptiness—especially in a patriarchal culture—will seek fulfillment through actual male partners and sons, or through serving the collective ideals of the animus in prostitution to the fathers. They will envy the penis and seek it to satisfy their longing for power; or they will try to lose their sense of impotence in worship of the man who gives sexual joy and the possibility of blissful merging. Awareness of the inner space can make a woman feel empty, lifeless, hollow, as if without food or substance—an oral cavity—due to lack of mother or lover. She then craves to be filled and is susceptible to abject dependency on an outer or animus impregnation. She can lose her own soul in the bliss of melting into her lover.

A woman's hunger to merge with the masculine as animus or outer man, her idealization of the masculine as true spirit to which she will submit, her need to be filled with patriarchal authority, or to be parented by the masculine, is changed through this inner intercourse. Too often there is no distinction felt between the unmothered woman's need for the mother and her need for a male partnership. Perhaps because so many women were nourished by the patriarchal animus of the caretaker, or because they found their brothers and fathers warmer or more valuable, they continue to seek strength and mothering from men and their own animus, even devaluing feminine nurturance when it is available for themselves.

Ereshkigal's stake fills the all-receptive emptiness of the feminine with feminine yang strength. It fills the eternally empty womb mouth, and gives a woman her own wholeness, so that the woman is not merely dependent on man or child, but can be unto herself as a full and separate individual. She can stand by her own No and Yes, her own solid stake. Ereshkigal's pole impregnates a woman with this new and holy attitude to life.

Thus the enstakement continues a process that permits the birth of the capacity to be separate and whole unto oneself in service to the dark goddess; the capacity to negate and to assert, to endure firmly grounded, to destroy and to create. The source is within, so there is no need for seeking validation indiscriminately or masochistically from the outside, nor for trying to make the environment friendly in order to get support, nor for appeasing others for reward. The basic need to be filled, so unmet by the mother in many modern women, finds a mode of satisfaction, and a standard of real sustenance and grounding is provided.

Our culture has clearly discouraged women from claiming impersonal feminine potency. The concept is considered monstrous; thus women are encouraged to be docile and to "relate with Eros" to sadistic paternal animus figures, rather than to claim their own equally sadistic-assertive power.

Such a *coniunctio* with the phallus of the goddess is not a substitute for the later marriage *coniunctio* between feminine and masculine, but it clarifies the lesser *coniunctio*, and makes a greater one possible—one that is genuine and passionate. For when a woman can feel her own individual self-connected stance she can be open to receive another into her own integral, strong vessel. The dreams of two women illustrate this:

I go to get my diagnosis because I am finishing analysis. The doctors tell me I have testes. I thought I had colitis. Now I see I don't have to be a handmaid to everyone. I've got balls and can create what I need.

I see that my mother, who is usually like a feminine doll and always puts herself down for her lovers, has also got a penis under her negligee. Now she can make love passionately. She is both woman and man.

This dream mother is like bearded Aphrodite, the hermaphroditic form of the love goddess. Both of these women had owned their own stake; they had their own viewpoint, and could begin to own their own creativity and individual and passionate connections to life.

Another woman, after telling her lover her own sense of reality and risking his separation from her, dreamt:

I visit a very old woman—like a witch. Two poisonous snakes she keeps get into my vagina. I am petrified and try to pull them out. She tells me that as long as they are together, they won't bite. I relax and feel a curious sense of safety. I know I will have to keep them together. The witch's daughter comes in and says she will help me.

Here the impregnating serpents are the opposites, which when united, as they are in Ereshkigal's abyss and on the archaic level of consciousness, and by a consenting, balanced ego vessel, can fertilize and protect. They will not destroy, but call forth a new "daugher" shadow, one the dreamer associated to "a woman who can be obnoxious, but she speaks her own word, and looks deep inside to find it."

All these women have begun to serve the dark feminine. They experience a new energy to stand firm on ground they feel belongs to their individually experienced reality itself—to stand against the collective, patriarchal animus, even if they are seen as obnoxious or unpolitic, even if they have to destroy the old sentimental forms of loving and the sense of well-being they once got from being merely agreeable and loyal and good and "healthy." For until the demonic powers of the dark goddess are claimed, there is no strength in the woman to grow from daughter to an adult who can stand against the force of the patriarchy in its inhuman form.

One woman who had begun to claim her potent affects, previously encapsulated in dream and bodily cysts, dreamt:

> A man molests his daughter with a huge phallus that he takes off [disconnected from his humanity] when he doesn't need it. His daughter is too small to talk about the terror she feels but she plays it out with dolls which a therapist can interpret.

Work on the dream led the woman to acknowledge memories of childhood abuses that she could not label or finish with and encapsulate in her usual animus-driven manner. Further musing led to the discovery that she still treated her own deep nonverbal emotions with the same contemptuous callousness her drunken father had manifested against her tender child self; in other words, her animus still tormented her.

Several women have expressed the felt difference between the yang strength of the goddess and the yang of the patriarchal, judgmental animus. One said: "There's a strength that feels like a womb with a penis in it—it does not cut only, but also nurtures and cares for me. It is strength for me, on some level." Unlike the animus yang power that "cuts only" or focuses with driving intensity or hits arrowlike from Apollonian distance, the feminine yang feels more embodied and firmly grounded. Yet also more diffuse. It maintains some relation to the whole gestalt through time and via sensed affect—while still seeing the parts objectively, and subordinated to the whole.[83]

Dream images of women who appear with phalluses or phallic objects penetrating the dreamer are more often than not associated with figures described as earthy, swarthy, demanding, getting their own way, strong, passionate—they are seen as inherently positive. Yet at first the nice, good, clean ego figure disdains and fears them as witchy or stinking, intuiting the inevitable dismemberment of the ego-ideal in order to encompass and claim such potencies. An example of this was provided by a woman who brought a dream:

> I am taken by a group of women [whom she identified as strong and outspoken individuals]. They are going to sacrifice me on a stone table. One of the women has a hump under her robe that turns out not to be a phallus but a huge knife.

She finished her recounting by exclaiming, "How could they do that to nice, little me?"—providing an example of how her sentimentalized persona feared and warded off her genuine self-assertion.

IV The Bipolar Goddess: Two Sisters

The Bipolar Goddess

I first came to the myth of Inanna's descent through a woman's initial dream: "I go under the water to the bottom of the sea to find my sister. She is hanging there on a meathook." This image suggested her necessity to search for qualities of the multifaceted, passionate and strong feminine suspended deep in the unconscious, and to return them to conscious life, for her sister is analogous here to Inanna and her own capacity for fruitful, trusting relatedness. She had lived with a sense of being alien and exiled as if in hell, and felt closer to Ereshkigal's dark realm than to the energies symbolized by the image of Inanna.

At first I understood the meathook as a vicious callousness, which we connected to family experience and to her animus. I did not find the Inanna amplification until the unpeeling of her schizoid defenses had been underway for two years, and she was well on her way into the underworld herself. I was grateful, then, for the myth's teaching that the terrible slowness of the process—gate by gate—was the right pace.

This woman had been identified with the values of the patriarchy. She was in graduate school, trying to be heroic and smart and charming. But she was full of anger and fear, and could only relate to men if they were homosexual. Her dream, as does the myth itself, suggests the necessity of connecting the upper-world feminine, whether pathologically compressed or healthy, with the underworld shadow. For before a woman can disidentify from the cycle, to reverence its wholeness pattern as transpersonal, she must suffer the death of her ego-ideal within it. Maintenance of this ideal is connected to repression of part of the feminine wholeness pattern in the underworld.

*

Ereshkigal is called Inanna's sister in the poem. She is her shadow, or complement: together the two goddesses make the bipolar wholeness pattern of the archetypal feminine, the

43

mother-daughter biunity of the Great Goddess. It is analogous to the star Inanna, above and below, for the youthful virgin goddess of love and of harlots "is with remarkable frequency 'equated' with the female uroboric goddess of the beginning."[84] The goddess of the Great Above symbolizes all the ways life energies engage actively with one another and flow together, including connections that are loving and disjunctions that are passionate. Below, and too often repressed, is the energy that turns back on itself, goes down into self-preserving introversions. It is the energy that makes a woman able to be separate unto herself, to survive alone.

Psychologically, we see these two energy patterns in the empathetic and self-isolating modalities that are basic to feminine psychology, in relation to all inner and outer partners—children, creative projects, lovers, even to a woman's own autonomous emotions and perceptions and thoughts. The active engagement that wants another, that wraps the partnership in an active loving and warring embrace—that is Inanna; the circling back and down, disinterested in the other, alone, even cold—that is Ereshkigal.[85]

It is not pathological to be inconstant, this myth tells us; rather it is a service to the bipolar goddess of life and transformation. Many women get caught in the separative part of the cycle and react negatively and guiltily to its seemingly ruthless coldness and they fall into depression. Or they cling to the related part, even when it feels false and a disservice to their own integrity (until the Self enforces its demands through unconscious coldness, feistiness, etc.), because they do not recognize the bipolar wholeness pattern.

We see this pattern in many pairs of goddesses: Athena and Medusa; heavenly Aphrodite and Uranian Aphrodite, the eldest of the fates; Mother Kali and devouring Kali-Durga; the light and dark side of the moon. We may consider these pairs as related to the two kinds of energy of the menstrual cycle, the ovulatory (white) and menstruating (red) phases.[86] The bifurcation often appears in dream images of patriarchially oriented women as a splitting of the female body into above and below the waist—the upper part suggesting the more nurturant and culturally and personally "good" and "related" sides of a woman; the lower for "ugly," "smelly," and impersonal "negative" aggressive and impassioned energies. Our cultural divisions have not the same content as do those of the Sumerians, for Inanna celebrated her vulva with open delight and relished her power. And even within our culture there are general and individual differences. What is repressed for those who are intellectual, achieving daughters of the patriarchy is not always what is devalued and ignored by those who are caught in the roles of mother and wife.

In relating to the images of the feminine presented in this myth, some women find themselves gripped by the erotic and active-assertive side of Inanna; they are able to feel their own previously feared energies mirrored in this upper-world goddess. It is as if they have to redeem the potential of joyful sexuality and/or active assertion from the underworld of their psyche. Other women, already comfortably conscious of their erotic and/or assertive capacities, may need to meet the potentials of patient receptivity and gestation imaged in the figure of Ereshkigal. They may have to "descend" temporarily from their accepted patterns of behavior into a period of introversion (or actual pregnancy or depression), in order to continue the process of realizing their potential wholeness.

But no matter how the pattern is imaged or incarnates, it is there, and it is bipolar, for alternation, the oscillating way, is a function of the feminine Self. Its experience is central to the inconstant, rhythmic quality of the feminine mode as it alternates through time, manifesting first one phase, then another. Both goddess images represent phases of one whole that needs to be seen and honored.

So this myth teaches us the life-enhancing *circulatio* pattern. Inanna marches into the underworld with determination, going actively and consciously towards her own sacrifice—just as modern woman has to acquiesce and cooperate in her introversion and necessary regressions into the underworld magic and archaic levels of consciousness. She must go down to meet her own instinctual beginnings, to find the face of the Great Goddess, and of herself before she was born to consciousness, into the matrix of transpersonal energies before they have been sorted and rendered acceptable. It is a sacrifice of what is above—to and for what is below. (From this perspective Inanna is a prefiguration of Christ and Odin. Or, incarnating through the planetary spheres into earth, she is an ancestress of the Gnostic Sophia.)

Incest With the Mother or Sister

I want to raise the theme of incest with the mother or sister, since it is clearly implied in the goddess' bipolarity. For a woman this connotes many things. In the present context it is a way of "incorporating the mother's dark powers rather than destroying or escaping them."[87] The erotic bond permits intimate connection to positive shadow qualities the woman may never have had conscious access to in herself. It is also a return to the possibility of being intimately reconnected to an other who is like herself and who can, therefore, validate her fully.

The mystery of love between mother and daughter, and between women who are equals, is implied. Anne Sexton wrote of "the cave of the mirror, that double woman who stares at herself," in her poem "The Double Image." A woman in therapy dreamt of "looking into a mirror and seeing another who is just like me, so I am valid and safe." As Adrienne Rich puts it, the "Mirror in which two are seen as one/She is the one you call sister."[88] Another woman repeatedly painted two sisters hugging each other, and "the two pressed together bodies look like one person." She explained: "Two sisters hugging make one person who is strong. And that is the way I can hug myself when I need to be mothered and there is no one else to do it. Me to me, like sister to sister." She wrote notes to her female therapist, calling her "sister." It is not linguistic formality alone that makes Inanna call Ereshkigal her sister.

This incest suggests uroboric nurture, the level of the symbiotic bond that confirms a woman in her self-worth and lets her go forth with her own feminine soul, free from bondage to the outer collective. It often involves the image of eating— even of eating the therapist—to take in the soul fragments that are still seen only in the mirror of the other one of the dyad. "I want you to just sit there quietly so I can eat you back into me," said one woman. Another imaged herself as "a self-devouring slug . . . hanging there below everything, just slowly taking in my anger and gluttony and sloth while you watch. Because I sense you've done that too." Like a uroboric pelican (the alchemical *circulatio* vessel), she felt she needed to consume her own previously shunned instincts. She still called them by the names she had used all her life to brand them sinful for she felt she first needed to accept their substance without idealization.

In therapy there is often an intense eroticized transference to the woman therapist when this level is touched—a uroboric merging that melts the animus defensiveness and permits rebirth with the capacity to express needs and feelings actively. One woman's active imagination involved making love to the female therapist, entering her while they fell through the floor into a deep pool below. She felt herself turn into liquid and dissolve in the therapist's warm body. After some time of blissful unconsciousness, she felt herself emerge as a two-inch-long infant, "like the baby who entered Mary's womb on a shaft of light." This infant could be nourished in the therapy. Such incest with the mother permits healing of the wounded animus-ego and its dissolution in the trusted therapeutic container, in order to allow the birth and nurturance of the Self-child as a new wholeness pattern.

As in all love relationships, a cross-fertilization is implied. Inanna brings differentiated awareness and activity to stir up Ereshkigal's realm, to effect a conscious suffering, perhaps a birth. In return she receives her own death and rebirth, the capacity to witness, and a new strength in introverted presence. Above ground Inanna is like a cornucopia, pouring forth, passionately initiating. Below she is passive, herself an initiate. She is dissolved and the receiver of life's processes— decay as an underworld gestation, not of child but of Being itself in its seemingly most negative mode. Simultaneously, Ereshkigal becomes active and aware. The cross-fertilization between the two goddesses has a profound effect on each of them and on their creative capacities; it ultimately changes the relationship between upper and lower worlds and creates a new masculine-feminine balance in the upper world.

In the analytic container such profound cross-fertilization occurs through the intense transference-countertransference inevitable when the work proceeds into the magic and archaic levels of the psyche. Typically, both parties are touched deeply through shared or complementary complexes and must relate to the archetypal energy patterns constellated through those sensitive spots. As Jung taught, both parties will emerge changed when the work is an initiatory descent, for both make the journey together. Even if the analyst has already been through much of the territory, there are new areas opened by each new analysand. So there are always new experiences and new insights, new surprises, new openings that go deeper or wider into the endless realm of the psyche.

There is another aspect of the incest with the mother that is frequently seen in the analysis of fathers' daughters who have actively repudiated weak mothers and over-identified with intellect and masculine spirit. Their mothers have been seen as the model of inferiority from which they have made every effort to escape. Then incest with the mother can be a painful awakening to qualities shared with the mother, an identity with the despised and derogated female. One woman, after exploring her father's shadow qualities and disentangling herself from identification with him, began to think about her mother. She was dismayed to realize, "I've repeated my mother's life. I thought I was like my father, his favorite. But I see I am like her. She was totally subservient, belonged to him, lived in servitude. We've both lost ourselves." Another, after returning from a visit to her parental home, despaired, "I'm just like her, cheap and mean, hating and trying to please, scared shitless. I thought I was so strong and intelligent and had got away from that." Another, who could only see her mother's negative shadow, began to examine her connection to the qualities she had felt hurtful to herself: "I have always hated her spoiling envy, but I see I am similar. She takes in stray people and shoves aside her own children, but I nourish my students and ignore my own needs. It's not so different."

In all these examples the personal mother is identical with the woman's negative shadow, which is seen in projection on the mother. Adult daughters of the father find it humiliating to see the bonds of weakness and self-hate which they share with their mothers. The insight nails them to reality, destroys their heroic, grandiose ego-ideal, and initiates a period of descent into depression as they suffer through their identity with the wounded, derogated feminine—in much the same way as Inanna rotted on the pole of the raped and derogated Ereshkigal.

Until the negative shadow qualities are seen in their wider cultural context, the daughter feels particularly cursed and hopeless. Here a feminist perspective is therapeutic. To see that all women have suffered cultural derogation means it is not one woman's fault that she felt weak and inadequate in her own life and in supporting her own daughter. The archetypal cultural perspective removes the onus from the particular mother, and with it from a cycle of unmet demands, of hurts, frustrations, and vengeances which can persist into old age and prevent self-acceptance. The feminist perspective seems to permit an attitude of sympathetic witnessing to Self and mother that restructures the problem and is analogous, as we shall see, to the action of Enki's mourners.

V Descent, Sacrifice, Transformation

Descent

The motif of descent is commonplace in Jungian work. (It applies equally though differently to both women and men, although I am here dealing only with women's experience of the process.)[89] We make descents or introversions in the service of life, to scoop up more of what has been held unconscious by the Self in the underworld, until we are strong enough for the journey and willing to sacrifice libido for its release. The hardest descents are those to the primitive, uroboric depths where we suffer what feels like total dismemberment. But there are many others imaged as descents into tunnels, the belly or womb, into mountains and through mirrors. Some of the easier ones we may need to have undergone, to loosen rigidities and raise energy, before we can risk the shattering descents to the depths of our primal wounds to work on the psychic-somatic level of the basic hurt.

These deepest descents lead to radical reorganization and transformation of the conscious personality. But, like the shaman's journey or Inanna's, they are fraught with real peril. Hopefully in therapy the therapist may "manage" and companion the descents with help from the unconscious, but some fall beyond the therapist's capacity or open into the unseen crevasses of psychotic episodes. All descents provide entry into different levels of consciousness and can enhance life creatively. All of them imply suffering. All of them can serve as initiations. Meditation and dreaming and active imagination are modes of descent. So too are depressions, anxiety attacks, and experiences with hallucinogenic drugs.

The causal meaning of Inanna's descent has puzzled scholars. In the earliest version of the myth it has nothing to do with raising Dumuzi-Tammuz, for she has not yet even sent him down. The later Ishtar versions suggest the goddess wants to raise the dead, and Ereshkigal's reaction to the intrusion of the queen of heaven implies the dark goddess' fear to lose something she has been holding onto, something that has been dead to the above world. It may even suggest her fear to confront herself with another level of consciousness and to feel her own misery, to come to an awareness of suffering.[90]

Scholars have been inclined to dismiss as a mere excuse Inanna's stated reason for her descent:

> My elder sister, Ereshkigal,
> Because her husband, the lord Gugalanna had been killed,
> To witness the funeral rites . . . so be it.[91]

But I think those words hold the truth: Inanna descends to witness the funeral rites of the lord Gugalanna.

The name Gugalanna means "great bull of heaven." The bull is a symbol of masculine primordial energy, the fertilizing power of nature. In Sumer the bull is connected to various local and sky gods. The primal god, An, is called "fecund breed-bull"[92] and "great, wild bull,"[93] and it was he who created the bull of heaven which Ishtar demanded to punish Gilgamesh's insult to her.[94] Nanna, the moon god, has the crescent horns that make him too a bull of heaven (later he is considered the god of cowherders). Enlil is also considered a "personification of force"[95] and of "the spring winds [that] bring nature back to life."[96] Enlil is the husband of Ninlil-Ereshkigal, and probably the Gugalanna of the poem. The bull is the earth sign of Taurus, the spring astrological sign opposite to Scorpio, a water sign. Sometimes Inanna-Ishtar is portrayed with scorpion men as her servants. She is also the embodiment of earth's fertility, and the bull may be emblematic of the masculine force that complements her. Certainly its death causes her a special concern in the Gilgamesh epic as well as in the Descent poem.

"The lord Gugalanna had been killed." Gugalanna is, I think, the underworld aspect of Enlil. The wording of the poem suggests that Inanna must witness the repressed shadow of the sky god—the fact that Enlil was rapist and banished to the underworld for his violence. The sky god fathers are not only pure and admirable. The patriarchal gods have an underside, a large shadow split off into the unconscious. The poem's image suggests that this shadow is bull-like passion, raw desire and power, sadistic bull-dozing violence, demonic bullying. That stubborn, bullish, defensive shadow of the gods is a fact of the patriarchy and its heroic ideals, ideals which overwhelm the feminine and struggle to control and hold their own in life, charging ahead, uncaring where they destroy playful sensitivity and empathetic relatedness. Inanna's descent implies her confrontation with this archetypal patriarchal shadow. She must see the limits of the fathers and be witness to what was repressed; she must refind Ereshkigal.

Psychologically for modern women, the death of the bull of heaven implies that what once sustained and fertilized the animus-ego can no longer function. The ancestral father principle has been depotentiated, and with it animus ideals and imperatives which functioned to provide identity to the father's daughter. The disidentification can occur in several ways. When she can look behind the façade of the idealized father as model, a woman can begin to see the human fragility which it concealed, and she can then be free of the compelling magnetism of the ideal. "What I thought was such strength and vitality and intelligence in my father turns out like the Wizard of Oz. He's just a little man behind the curtain who could barely manage his business, trying to puff himself up," said one woman as she confronted the facts of her personal father's life. Another dreamt of her father as an Inquisitor, and was able to look at the archetypal shadow behind the Christian virtues her minister father had instilled in her. She said with astonishment and intensity as she confronted the dream image, "They burned women." For the first time she could look at the sadism involved in the patriarchal ideals she had worshipped, and see them as enemy of the feminine and herself.

When a daughter of the fathers sees the confusion and irrelevance, to her own personality, of the virtues and concepts which have hitherto sustained her, she can also begin to let them go, using the clear eye of Ereshkigal's objectivity. One woman imaged her father's lack of consistency as a locket she had had to wear, with the chaotic panoply of labels her father had given her swinging from its circumference. The wind blew them whimsically forward to be read. She could see the words had little to do with her reality, but she felt a genuine loss, and mourned the end of a system of identity that had given her life meaning. The meaning was not grounded in reality— she dreamt of giant girders suspended in the sky, endangering her—but the illusion had seemed to nourish her life. Confronting its loss is for a daughter of the fathers like mourning a death. In the ensuing depression, she must go below her adherence to ideals that have raped the feminine and separated above from below. She is forced to introvert and to offer herself as sacrifice to suffer the dismembering dissolution of her own old identity. In this way she follows Inanna.

Inanna's Death-Marriage

To witness the death of the bull of heaven brings the goddess to her descent. The next part of the myth implies her death-marriage—her death and impalement on the phallic post of the dark goddess, her incest with the yang side of the mother. In the myth Inanna goes down as if dressed for a wedding, even wearing the ointment "Let him come, let him come" on her eyes, and the breastplate "Come, man, come" on her body. She seems to want at first to use her seductive powers to try to raise the dead, to reanimate the bull of heaven. But she goes as "witness" of the funeral rites, "so be it," as if also acquiescing to what she clearly knows will happen to herself. It is her funeral, also, and she prepares for it. Thus she can open herself to receive the potent forces dormant in the underworld. Like any initiate, she courageously surrenders to her own sacrifice, in order to gain new power and knowledge.[97] Like the seed which must die in order to be reborn, the goddess of the granary submits. Like the good metal and good stone and good boxwood of the poem, which are broken by craftsmen in their creative process,[98] Inanna allows herself to be broken for a new creation.

Sacrifice and Energy Exchange

Sacrifice is the basis of primordial fertility rites. Inanna offers herself in sacrifice, witnessing to the death of fertility and bringing herself as seed. She offers her own libido to replenish the lost source. Hers is the voluntary immolation upon which continual creation depends. As Eliade points out:

> The myth of the birth of edible plants...always involves the spontaneous sacrifice of a divine being. This may be a mother, a young girl, a child or a man....[In this extremely widespread mythological motif] the fundamental idea is that life can only be born of another life which is sacrificed; the death by violence is creative in the sense that the sacrificed life becomes manifest...at another level of existence. The sacrifice brings about a gigantic change.[99]

The rites of the earth mother involve a *hierosgamos* and/or violent death. In the collective rituals the one sacrificed is the scapegoat of the community. The victim is offered to the earth goddess in order that she bestow "good crops, seasons, and health."[100] It is "the sowing which fecundates the Earth-Mother."[101] According to Erich Neumann:

> The mother's sacrifice of the male, her son, was preceded in earlier times by a sacrifice of the daughter.... The victim is a woman and on another day a young girl, playing the part of earth goddess [as the corn]; she is beheaded, and her blood is sprinkled on fruit, seeds, and so on, to guarantee their increase. ... The essential elements in this fertility ritual are the beheading of the woman as goddess, the frucitfying sacrifice of her blood, the flaying of her body, and the investment of the... priest in her skin.[102]

Such rituals were widespread. There is evidence that they took place in ancient Mexico, among the Pawnees,[103] and probably among the forerunners of the Sumerians. Perhaps the immolation of pigs in Athens, and their dismemberment when they had become fertilizing rotten flesh, is a later adaptation of this same necessity to sacrifice of the earth to the earth that new life may rise.

We know that when Inanna was in the underworld, nothing grew or copulated. The earth was barren. The goddess had withdrawn in sacrifice to herself: the first scapegoat. From the perspective of this sacrifice we can see that Inanna maintains the balance of life. From "highest heaven" she goes to "earth's deepest ground." To the extent that she was high, she must go low; from extraverted, active, to inert passive meat; from differentiated and ideal to undifferentiated and primordial. Only thus can the balance demanded by the Great Round be maintained. It is an exchange of libido for the purpose of renewal.

We can see from this myth that the original scapegoat had nothing to do with a sin offering. Ethics were not involved; only the necessity that exists under the natural law of the conservation of energy to maintain a balance of energy in the overall system of life. Nothing changes or grows without the food of some other sacrifice. This is the basis of women's experience of childbearing and of all blood mysteries that create and maintain life. It is known to matriarchal consciousness and to modern physics. It is the basis of psychology and transformation of any kind, and Jung's libido theory is based upon this profound and cosmic fact.

The myth of Inanna's descent and return is centered on this archetype of exchanging energy through sacrifice. It reveals a complex pattern: the bull of heaven is killed; earth loses its fertilizing principle and is recompensed through the immolation of the goddess; Innanna becomes the meat of the underworld, its food and rotting fertilizer, which in turn is ransomed from Enki's sources. The rise of the goddess must be paid for by the birth of something monstrous from Ereshkigal,[104] by suffering and eventually by the descent of a substitute offering. Finally Dumuzi is partially redeemed to the upper world by the sacrifice of his sister. Libido runs from one pattern to another in this archetypal exchange. No part is static. It is all in process—death, sacrifice, decay, rebirth—as part of the dynamism of life's Great Round.

Psychologically, the processual aspect of the exchange is experienced as painful and slow. We feel identified with whatever aspect we are closest to and can rarely find the partial relief provided in moments of enlightenment when we can see the pattern from a transcendent perspective. Although our depressions and the sacrifice of our incomplete ideals and illusions are modes of rendering an exchange of libido, analogous to the ritual of the myth, the process feels agonizing and is made worse when we blame ourselves for being depressed. We are forced to offer what we hold dear, what we have paid much to gain. And we cannot even know that the loss will be recompensed in the ways we desire. The sacrifice may change the balance of energy somewhere in the overall psychic system where we did not even want a change. All we can know is that finding renewal and connection with the potent forces of the underworld will involve breaking up the old pattern, the death of a gestalt we were comfortable with on some level, the death of a seemingly whole identity. We will rarely approach such dismemberment if our pain is not already severe.

That Inanna needs to restore herself in her underworld aspect is implied in the notion of the bipolarity in the one energy field of the goddess. (Thus Hera retires to her yearly rejuvenating, revirginating bath.) More specifically and psychologically, for a daughter of the fathers, the necessity for descent is implied in Inanna's lament to the sky god about her homelessness. She had been dispossessed, lost the focus of her self-acclaim and self-acceptance. She needs to sacrifice her dependence on the patriarchal gods to find her true home in the basic feminine and processual ground of being. For, as daughter, sister, hierodule of the male sky gods, she has suffered the diminishment of her own potency that many of us know (and even enjoy) when we relate primarily to and through our masculine partners and our animus.

One poem tells us that Inanna gave up her own choice of the farmer god as her husband in order to accept the shepherd, Dumuzi, because her brother the sun god urged the match.[105] Inanna did not stand her own objective feeling ground. She was persuaded. Perhaps that was inevitable or even necessary for her. But as hetaera (companion) who dispenses and serves the joys of life and the masculine gods, she is ever endangered by losing herself through fostering subservient connectedness. She needs to return to the dark, unacceptable feminine goddess to renew her own potency; not to use it as defensive armoring shield—as Athena reconnected to the gorgon and wore its fearful face—but restructured, reborn in an inner process and connected to the full range of feminine instinctual patterns.

Descent as Controlled Therapeutic Regression

What I have seen and experienced in myself and other women who are successful daughters of the collective, often unmothered daughters of the animus and the patriarchy, is that we suffer a basic fault (Michael Balint's term). We do not have an adequate sense of our own ground nor connection to our own embodied strength and needs adequate to provide us with a resilient feminine, balanced yin-yang, processual ego. There is a fault in the basic levels of our personality—a deep split, maintained by loyalty to superego ideals that no longer function to enhance life, a loyalty that keeps the ego alienated from reality, in a regressed, inflated, Self-identified mode. Thus we need to undergo a "controlled regression" into the borderland-underworld levels of the dark goddess—back to ourselves before we had the form we know, back to the magic and archaic levels of consciousness and to the transpersonal passions and rages which both blast and nurture us there;

back to the body-mind, and the preverbal tomb-womb states, searching back to the deep feminine, the "dual mother" Jung writes about.[106]

On the way down we shed the identifications with and the defenses against the animus, introverting to initially humiliating and devastating, but ultimately safer, primal levels. There we may learn to survive in a different way and to await the chance for rebirth. Sometimes we wait a long time, caught in coming to know our primal beginnings from a new perspective, feeling loosened from old meanings as if suspended out of life. In the depths of the underworld the opposing, chaotic energies of the Great Round battle in us while we feel ourselves to be without energy. They dismember the old animus-ego complex and its faulty identifications.

Work on this level in therapy involves the deepest affects and is inevitably connected to preverbal, "infantile" processes. The therapist must be willing to participate where needed, often working on the body-mind level where there is as yet no image in the other's awareness and where instinct and affect and sensory perception begin to coalesce first in a body sensation, which can be intensified to bring forth memory or image. Silence, affirmative mirroring attention, touch, holding, sounding and singing, gesture, breathing, nonverbal actions like drawing, sandplay, building with clay or blocks, dancing— all have their time and place.

On this magic and matriarchal level the elements of ritual are potent and need to be respected, even encouraged. The gestures and enactments of psychodrama can be helpful to create or recreate a space, an emotion, a meaning, an archetypal pattern. But mainly the therapist must be guided by the powerful affective connections of the transference-countertransference, and by the images of dream and fantasy, to sense where and how the process wants to go. The therapeutic attitude is one of actively allowing each individual to be with him or herself in any way necessary. This may lead to all kinds of creative improvisations—actions and gestures and permissions, both symbolic and literal—to touch the regressed and hidden pre-ego, and to help it to learn to feel valid and to trust.

Such maternally nurturant and companioning behavior has profound effects, although these are often kept secret or left unspoken. Their impact may be revealed only in dream images, or years later reported as turning points in the work. Often part of the effect is due to the patient's or analysand's feeling that such acceptance and participation go beyond conventional parameters of verbal therapy and, therefore, suggest the therapist's willingness to "be unorthodox"—even defying some superego prohibitions. This seems to make the other feel deeply allied with and validated on the archaic-matriarchal level. An analyst—serving as the carrier of archetypal projections—must accept the other's deeply individual feelings and needs, caring more for them than for abstract and impersonal collective conventions.

*

Jung writes of the descent to the plant level as "the downward way, the yin way ... [to] earth, the darkness of humanity."[107] It is to this descent that the goddess Inanna and we modern women must submit, going into the deep, inchoate places where the extremes of beauty and ugliness swim or dissolve together in a paradoxical, seemingly meaningless state. Even the queen of beauty becomes raw, rotten meat. Life loses its savor. But it is a sacred process—even the rot—for it represents submission to Ereshkigal and the destructive-transformative mysteries that she symbolizes.

VI   Unveiling and Passing through the Gates

Unveiling

The process by which the stellar goddess submits herself to concreteness and incarnation involves her unveiling. This motif suggests the removal of old illusions and false identities that may have served in the upper world, but which count for nothing in the Netherworld. There one stands naked before the all-seeing eyes of the dark goddess. The unveiling means being stripped bare, the unveiling of the goddess to herself— the original striptease. It suggests a need to be utterly exposed, undefended, open to having one's soul searched by the eye of death, the dark eye of the Self.

Jung writes that often "undressing symbolizes the extraction of the soul."[108] He quotes an alchemical text: "Disrobe me, that mine inner beauty may be revealed."[109] The inner beauty is the soul, child of sun and moon. But, adds Jung, "undressing signifies putrefaction" as well, and in alchemy "the *nigredo* is also represented as the 'garment of darkness.'"[110]

So both putrefaction and the extraction of the soul are symbolized by undressing, for clothing is the flesh of incarnation and death is the taking off of the mortal vestment. Undressing for human beings—already incarnated in body-egos— is a disincarnation mode, the end of one form of body-ego existence and the revelation of the hidden Self. On the other hand, for the stellar goddess and for inadequately incarnated daughters of the father, unveiling is a mode of embodying soul in earthly matter.

Unveiling also relates to exhibitionism—a necessary going naked before the goddess. For us it often means stripping before the Self and thus we feel so exposed, especially when parents and others who first embodied the Self mocked us in early life. And yet it is daring this exposure which permits validation of the body-ego before the Self or the Great Mother. Revealing all, we find her objective acceptance of all of us. We have been seen and thus can exist. But we must unveil and exhibit ourselves naked.

Such unveiling is immensely hard for a daughter of the

59

fathers (and it is probably no accident that Athena was born in full armor), for it means giving up both defensiveness and the illusions of identity provided by the regalia of the upper world, those roles and marks of power and status earned from the patriarchy which serve as surrogate, persona-identity to a woman who is handmaid to the fathers and the animus.

For therapists working on the deepest levels such unveiling is also essential. It permits us to be penetrated by the reality of the other, the full force of the affects, without defending ourselves with our professional persona. Only thus can we orient honestly by inner, experienced reality. Only thus can we avoid isolating the other in a false subjectivity that feels hellish, as when we throw back everything as projection. In the realm of the dark feminine there is no possibility of hiding. We are found out by our dreams and by our own reverberating complexes. On the deep levels of the transference-countertransference, outer and inner merge and two individuals share one psychic reality in the field force of *participation mystique;* hence it is often hard to discern what affect or image belongs to whom. This, the myth tells us, is part of the law of the underworld: those who descend must disrobe. Analyst and analysand meet in one deep container to suffer the death-marriage-transformation demanded by the goddess.

The esoteric meaning of unveiling, and the Eastern one, as the Bhagavad-Gita tells us, is the casting off of identities: "Even as a person casts off worn clothes and puts on new, so the indwelling being casts off worn bodies and enters into others that are new." The descent and return of the goddess Inanna, like the Eleusinian mysteries, conveys the message of unquenchable indwelling life. Scholars think that the Sumerians and Akkadians did not believe in reincarnation, although the Akkadian Ereshkigal kept the water of life and used it to restore Inanna's corpse. The motif has perhaps more to do with rebirth and reillumination of consciousness. Inanna sheds her old identities, is reduced to primal matter, and then is reborn. Similarly, individuals undergoing initiations in a sacred process shed their old identities and enter new ones. The unveiling is part of the initiation process.

There may also lie, in this unveiling motif, some suggestion of the preparatory stages for temple prostitution. Like modern nuns, divested of their secular identity, so the priestesses of

Inanna's temples may have undergone a similar process—even to dying in the initiation on the cross of the impersonal phallus of any man, which opened them to experience their sexuality as an aspect of their service to the goddess.

From yet another perspective, the disrobing of Inanna suggests her—and the initiate's, following her—awareness of different levels of consciousness. The seven garments of queenship lie on her body at the levels of the kundalini chakras. She wears crown, rod or ear pendants (in different versions of the myth), necklace, breast stones, gold ring or hip girdle, bracelets, and a garment of ladyship (called breechcloth in the Akkadian version). As she divests and reinvests herself of these objects attention may have been called to the corresponding chakra.[111] She is brought down to naked *muladhara* —the rigid, inert material of incarnation, the bare ground of facts and bodily reality; down from the crown with its blissful uniting of opposites (Inanna as the goddess presiding over such relations) and cosmic consciousness into the pelvis; down to the root chakra where potential life sleeps and is restored in another paradoxical uniting of opposites.

The Gates

The seven gates of Ereshkigal's house have analogies in Egyptian material. Neumann describes "the seven dwellings of the underworld . . . [as] seven aspects of the Feminine."[112] The female gate guardians in Egypt he calls "manifestations of the Great Goddess in her predominately terrible aspect."[113] Such differentiation of the monsters of the Sumerian-Akkadian underworld took place well after the Descent myth was written. Here there is only one gatekeeper, Neti. The gates are perhaps more accurately related to the seven planetary positions with which the planet Inanna-Ishtar would move into conjunction on her descent and return; the Sumerians kept accurate astronomical observations of planets, including Venus returns,[114] each with its different metallic and psychological correlations.[115] To go more deeply into the specific meanings of the gates here would lead too far afield—into the psychology of the chakras and the planets, their symbolic and instinctual meanings and the therapist's role in dealing with their energies.

The gates are also stages of an initiatory and sacrificial way like stations of the Cross. As a motif they may appear in modern dream material in many guises. One woman dreamt of an innocent Marilyn Monroe figure falling through seven balconies to a bloody death. The dream presaged a severe depression and the dreamer's introduction to eruptive primal affects that opened her into the depths of her psyche. Another dreamt of having to strain her urine through seven sieves. She said, "I need to be careful in layering down to the den of flames. My feelings will erupt and destroy everything." She saw her analytic process as a potential descent into hell, where her tidy controls would no longer serve her life. The care with which her process allowed her to descend made the work less precipitous than that of the first dreamer, and reassured her that her psyche permitted a pace fitted to her necessity.

VII Witnessing and the Search for Wisdom

Ninshubur

Before her descent Inanna prepared the strategy for her rescue, and instructed Ninshubur to carry it out if she did not reappear from her journey after three days. She had foreknowledge that she would need help if she got stuck in the underworld—a motif familiar from many mythologies and from clinical practice.

Ninshubur, the trusted executive of Inanna, provides evidence of the priestly organization of the Sumerian gods' and goddesses' temples. They were staffed much as households. Ninshubur, whose name means Queen of the East, was the female handmaid or vizier of the Great Goddess. She is the earthly, executive arm of Inanna, called upon whenever the goddess needs assistance for her needs and projects. She leads the royal bridegroom to the bed of the goddess, and when Inanna beguiled the *me,* the ordering principles of the world, from Enki by making him drunk, the goddess called upon Ninshubur to ensure their safe passage to her Erech temple. Ninshubur also warded off the fierce emissaries the wisdom god sent after Inanna to retrieve the *me.*

In the Descent myth Ninshubur is the one to whom Inanna entrusts her rescue. She is the servant who cries out after her mistress is missing for three days in the underworld, clamoring to men and women, then interceding with the sky gods for intervention on the goddess' behalf.

Psychologically, she seems to embody that small part of us that stays above ground while the soul descends, the still conscious and functioning aspect of the psyche which can witness the events below and above and feel concern for the fate of the soul. It is the part in therapy open to feeling and taking responsibility for action and understanding while most of the patient's energy is below in the unconscious, the part capable of sustaining the therapeutic alliance. It is analogous to the remarkable, strong, humble, functioning consciousness that can permit life to continue, can prevent a psychotic episode and total loss of soul, that can persist in its journey to find what is necessary. It is the spokeswoman of the Self, the

63

one who has heard Inanna, who keeps track of the days, and who cries out of her deep feeling that the goddess must be roused. Ninshubur, for me, is a model of woman's deepest, reflective-of-the-Self, priestess function, one which operates as simple executrix of the Self's commands, often when the soul is most threatened.

In the poems mentioning her, Ninshubur has no life of her own, no specificity beyond her capacity to serve. She simply carries out precisely and competently what the goddess asks of her. In her profound, egoless obedience, she is almost invisible —indeed she dresses like a beggar at Inanna's bidding. Yet on the "faithful servant" Ninshubur's integrity and reverence and capacity for action depend the turning in the myth, the turning which restores the reborn Inanna to the world of the Great Above. As the goddess says in the poem, "It is she who saved my life."[116]

A woman called her therapist to report that she was feeling suicidal and had found herself consuming and vomiting a large chocolate cake. She had become aware in therapy that her ravenous behavior was a way to nourish herself when she felt hurt and could dimly connect her current anguish to her fear of rejection by a male authority figure. Beginning to disidentify from her habitual pattern of impulsive, unconscious acting-out of her guilt, she felt desperate—so desperate that she decided to call her therapist, although "telephoning was abjectly dependent and humiliating." Such witnessing and overt asking for help was a new behavior for her—one that revealed her nascent Ninshubur function, the capacity to see and act on behalf of her own soul's value and its need.

Search through the Wrong Sources

Inanna tells Ninshubur to go first to the sky god, Enlil, the high father of all, then to Nanna-Sin, her own father, the moon god, then to Enki. Why does she not send Ninshubur to her mother or to Ninhursag, the earth mother? The poets of her culture saw Inanna, already and unfortunately, valuing masculine power more than that of the mothers. Perhaps it is because she is the gods' hierodule, or perhaps she feels their greater cultural potency. In any case, in her search for the necessary attitude to help her in extremis, she is wrong in her first choices. She seeks at first in seemingly powerful, but actually incapable or ungiving sources.

We see this search for help from the wrong sources often enough in therapy when patients insist on appealing to those who will reject them on principle (saying "such needs are infantile"), or out of world view or typological or consciousness level differences. Because the powerful parental archetype was initially projected onto those who could not adequately validate the individual, the seeker continues to expect help from such ungiving sources. Only after trying repeatedly, and staying stuck in the hell of feeling deprived and resentful, or even of turning against the need impulse itself (by identifying with the aggressive collective god, the superego), can such individuals learn to turn away.

Indeed, much of therapy involves learning to abandon the old patterns and to learn to turn towards truly nourishing and truly self-validating sources. Only in the process of learning to fill the archetypal parental structure with a new content, can a person realize that it is not his or her need or appetite for life that is at fault, but the fact that it was aimed towards the wrong source.

The two sky and moon gods refuse to and/or dare not rescue Inanna from the place of stuckness and death in the underworld. They embody impersonal patriarchal respect for law and order, too far away from the modality of both their "daughter" Inanna and the dark feminine. They see Inanna as merely ambitious, one who "craves" too much. They see her through the projection of their own bull-like shadow. And they cite the rule that "one who goes to the Great Dwelling stays there."[117] They seem almost spiteful, glad she got her comeuppance. In just such a way do the superego and those living by its tidy laws retaliate against, or abandon, those individuals and appetites daring to move beyond collective, conventional confines. There is no help for the wayward from the powers in control.

The Moon God

It is interesting that the moon god, Nanna-Sin, so often written of as lord of women, in this myth cares little for Inanna's plight. In Sumer Nanna is described as the power of lighting the night, measuring time, providing fertility of the marsh water, reeds, and herds. He is also an administrator and judge in the Netherworld at the time of the dark of the moon. But above the horizon he is less orderly. He is said to have married his wife Ningal ("the great lady," goddess of reeds) impetuously, without asking her father Enki for consent.[118]

Nanna is also connected to the kings of Ur. Periodic lustrations and sacred marriages are part of his cult. In general he is disinterested in his children. He is distant, moving in his own rhythms, and his children are unrelated to them. In one myth Utu (the sun god, Inanna's brother) and Inanna are even described as being seduced to the side of his enemies to bring about an eclipse of their father, the moon. The siblings are, by contrast, very close: Utu influences his sister's choice of husband (although the herdsman Dumuzi's bounty is said to be due to the fertilizing effect of the moon).

For Inanna the father principle is not mediated by a personal relationship. There is even the suggestion of antagonism between father and daughter. This has much to do with the rivalry between the cities of Ur and Erech and their titular deities, but it also suggests some of the psychological problems in being daughter of a lunar father. In the myth Nanna merely parrots the words of the high father, Enlil. He is jealous for his own power and brightness, yet unconsciously sides with abstract, senex rule. He defensively and contemptuously ignores his daughter, too deeply involved with his thin, wifely anima, the reed goddess Ningal and his own changes, lustrations, and productivity.

The daughters of such puer fathers often arrive in analysis with a façade of self-sufficiency—female heroes, with a driven but bound-up seductiveness. They despair of earning their father's attention except temporarily and unconsciously, often as a sexual object, and they are caught in having to defend themselves while trying to prove themselves equal and worthy of their father's praise. They split off their sensuousness, capture men and/or accomplishments, but feel no tenderness and little self-regard. They are focussed forever on seeking the father's blessing and personal attention, even trying to eclipse him in order to earn such necessity. They call out to him in multitudinous ways, always expecting the rejection of his cool, narcissistic disinterest.

VIII Empathetic-Creative Consciousness

Enki: God of Water, Wisdom, and Creativity

There is one "father" in the Descent myth who is helpful: Enki. His name means "lord of the earth" (like Poseidon). He is the wily water and wisdom god, ruling the flow of seas and rivers. He lives deep in the abyss. In several myths he is especially close to Inanna. In this myth he initiates the process of her release.

Enki is a remarkable divinity. In Sumer his waters were equated with the engendering power of semen and amniotic fluid.[119] On cylinder seals (as Ea, his later, Akkadian form) he is represented with a flowing water jar. That representation suggests the constellation of the Water Bearer, Aquarius; but Enki is more generally equated with Capricorn, the fish-goat,[120] who can traverse the depths and heights and is the true complement of the Great Mother in her sign of Cancer. Thus he shares a bond with both Ninhursag (who was originally called Ki—earth—Enki's ancient counterpart) and with Ereshkigal.

Enki is the generative, creative, playful, empathetic male. Like Mercurius he includes the opposites and has no abstract boundedness to the principle of law. Although Enki is said to have created the *me*, those ordering principles of the upper world and civilization, his order is creative, not static and preservative. He is the culture bringer, not the preserver of the status quo. His wisdom is that of improvisation and empathy. And having a bisexual breadth (in one myth he was said to undergo an eightfold pregnancy) he can penetrate into any necessity—even into the underworld. "Only . . . consciousness [of both sexes] can penetrate into the invisible world of Thanatos and all those psychic components of human nature that derive from death."[121] Enki's consciousness is like that of the second chakra, *svadhisthana*, where "trust in life and the self is the wisdom of the maternal waters." The trust, fluidity, ecstacy, and lubricating acceptance of what is—qualities of the

67

second chakra's mode of consciousness—can "heal the static
ills of the first [chakra]" and of the power-bound third.[122]
Enki's wisdom flows with, breaks up; it releases the inertia
and rigidity of the underworld. His waters are those in Sumerian myth that oppose the desert goddess. *Kur,* called Ereshkigal's realm, is also a word for desert. They are the waters
that restore the wasteland, symbolic of the never-ending flow
of life's energies.

Like the flow of libidinous affect, these waters carry us
back into life after a deathlike depression. One woman expressed her experience of this return:

> I will not hold myself in. I will let flow, let rip, be obnoxious.
> I'll let my reactions out. And so what. Take it or leave it. [She
> paused] Just saying that lets something change. I can feel a
> flowing with. All those needs and jealousy. Feels so strange,
> like breathing deeply. It might be a cure for my dead, dry
> place.... And also, such waters never stop as long as there's
> life in me. There's no end to piss and spit.

And so her passions opened and could be expressed, because
she could stop protecting herself in the old, inhibited ways.
She could trust her analyst to receive the flow. She could give
up her learned inhibition, her need to take care of her caretaker.

This flowing is part of the energy symbolized by Enki's
waters. He is also the creative sculptor god, called "image
fashioner" and god of craftsmen and artists, "god of the original form, archetype."[123] He is one of the creators of men—in a
contest with the earth goddess in which they made various
forms of human life from clay, when she created deformities,
he found roles in life for them to fill. Endlessly, he improvises
to create what the moment needs. He cares little for the rules
and precedents of the high-principled patriarchal gods, and is
thus often called upon to get them out of difficult impasses; in
many poems he provides the source of rescue, or he con-
quers the chaos they fear. Often he mediates between the
world of the fathers and the feminine. Always he flows creatively with life, and therefore holds the possibility of totally
restructuring the system from his own impetus. In the Descent
myth he cracks the inertia of the legalistic-defensive paradigm
by a totally new approach. Rather than abiding by the prece-

dents and laws, he initiates a new process, and he does so by resorting to what was hitherto ignored: he moves with feeling.

He takes some dirt from under his red-painted fingernail,[124] insignificant, rejected, even previously invisible stuff, remnant of the larger creative process. Earth is the element of *muladhara* and Ereshkigal. It is the embodied stuff which corresponds to the energy of matter and the meat Inanna had become in the underworld. It is also the silt of Enki's riverbeds, the clay that was the primary building material of Sumer's cities and of the tablets on which cuneiform writing was preserved. It is the material through which Sumerian culture incarnates and witnesses. In myth it is what men and women were created from.

In the analytic process this dirt is analogous to the *prima materia*—unpremeditated, raw, basic reactiveness, open to all possibilities because it is of the same stuff as the creator god's creative medium. It is thus the basic emotional material of the analytic process, as of all life. Its vast potency is hidden in the small, potent, autonomous flickers of emotion, the gripping, vibrant, and painful concrete details, the compelling fantasies that nearly slipped by or were concealed. The dirt under the nail is like the autonomous psyche as it is revealed in the small, personal, here-and-now, affect-laden facts that are not grand and proof of effective performance in ways the superego would prefer, but the despised slag of life's processes: solid, subtle, and capable of radically changing the analytic perspective.

Figures Who Mirror the Dark Goddess

With the dirt from under his fingernail Enki creates two little servant-mourner figures, a *kalatur* and a *kurgarra.* These are described as "sexless devotees"[125] or "creature[s] neither male nor female."[126] They are perhaps hermaphroditic or androgynous, polymorphous creatures, who participate in the Great Round by their own lack of sexual differentiation. The opposites, male and female, are not yet set apart in them. Thus they do not embody consciousness as discrimination based upon cutting apart, separation, and standing adversary, but consciousness as empathy and mirroring. So they can creep up to Ereshkigal, unchallenged through all the gates—"like flies, they flew through the cracks in the doors."[127] They are humble, nonheroic creatures, without definition or even the need to be separately defined, without any sense of what we would call ego-needs. These little asexual creatures represent the attitude necessary to draw a blessing from the dark goddess.

What they are told to do by Enki is just what therapists do in those abyss places that are preverbal and primal, where psyche and body meet on the borderline, where all is timeless and spaceless and the patterns of the magic level of consciousness hold.[128] These creatures move in close to the goddess, ignoring the ways of upper-world law and distance. Then they witness and they mirror with empathy, rather than inflationary identification which loses all sense of the separateness of I and Thou. Theirs is a created capacity. They see and feel, and they groan with. Honoring the goddess, they express the suffering of existence that Ereshkigal now feels; for consciousness has come into her realm and with it consciousness of pain. They affirm her in her suffering. They have been taught by Enki to trust the life force even when it sounds its misery.

Complaining is one voice of the dark goddess. It is a way of expressing life, valid and deep in the feminine soul. It does not, first and foremost, seek alleviation, but simply to state the existence of things as they are felt to be to a sensitive and vulnerable being. It is one of the bases of the feeling function, not to be seen and judged from the stoic-heroic superego perspective as foolish *qvetching* and passive whining, but just as autonomous fact—"that's the way it is." Enki's wisdom teaches us that suffering with is part of reverencing.

Enki's mourners moan with Ereshkigal. When she says, "Woe! Oh my inside!" they echo her with, "Woe! You who sigh our queen. Oh, your inside!" When she says, "Woe! Oh my outside!" they echo her with, "Woe! You who sigh our queen. Oh, your outside!"[129] Their echoing makes a litany, transforms the pain into poetry and prayer. It makes out of life's dark misery a song of the goddess. It establishes art as a reverent and creative and sympathetic response to the passions and pains of life. And it shows the potency of such a litany. For with their mirroring song they ransom a goddess of life. From Ereshkigal pours forth not more destruction but generosity. The goddess of nature is grateful for the humble mirroring, for hearing the song of herself. Precisely empathetic expression itself moves her. She answers the little creatures:

> Who ever you are,
> [Because] you have said: From my inside to your inside,
> From my outside to your outside,
> If you are gods, I shall pronounce a [kindly] word for you,
> If you are men, I shall decree a [kindly] fate for you.[130]

We see this transformation occur in therapy when misery is accepted and affirmed. Two women expressed their sense of the transformation:

> How can you stand me? All I do is complain. I give you nothing. Everything you offer I reject, even the space to be myself. [And some time after speaking, the patient dared to fall asleep, finally trusting the therapist's acceptance.]

> I can cry alone. That's easy. It's crying with.... I don't want answers, just someone to sit with me when I cry. That turns something over inside me. I feel hope and life return from deep within—like the faint bubbling of a spring—first almost frozen, then muddy, then a tiny rivulet.

Inside and Outside

The terminology of Ereshkigal and the mourners is significant —inside and outside. It defines a border region that is one of the earliest parameters of awareness in childhood. This is a border most unclear in the deepest layers of the mother complex. For inner and outer tend to merge and flow on the magic level of consciousness and within the symbiotic bond (as when the mother experiences the child's needs as her own and the child picks up the mother's unconscious emotions). We see this analytically in projective identification of transference-countertransference reactions. Indeed, I and Thou are so fluid within this field of *participation mystique* that there is often no clear sense of objectivity and difference between the psychic boundaries of two persons. Rather there is a sense of union and intimacy that can be tuned into with subtle intuitive and kinesthetic perceptions.

The border between inside and outside, I and Thou, is the first and final and most mysterious gate of Ereshkigal's house.

It is the place of the osmotic membrane between child and mother, self and other, self and the gods. It is the gate beyond (or out of) and into incarnated existence as we know it: the gate of birth—when what was inside and merged comes forth —and the gate of death—when what was separate returns. It is analogous to the horizon where Inanna as star brings dawn and twilight. And it is the place of crossing where two becomes one and one becomes two. For us to experience the flow of sensed identity across and unbounded is to be nurtured in the archaic consciousness, uroboric bliss, that permits life to flower and consciousness to expand or dissolve. To flow into awareness of the border is to begin to find one's own separate ground of being. Often when we experience this border it is with a consciousness born of suffering and loss. Either we are aware of the loss of bliss and merger when we pass through to our sense of separateness, or we may experience the loss of individual autonomy when we merge or are swallowed up or dissolve in a larger container. But we cannot exist without both experiences.

Feminine receptive consciousness does not experience the border as a tidy boundary separating what is sensed as "me" from what is sensed as "not-me." The border is not a fixed barrier demarcating a clear sense of individual identity in opposition to the other, who is felt to be the object of heroic action. Rather the border is permeable, easily penetrated by empathic sensing of the other, a capacity to feel with and to share the other's emotional presence.

An individual who has felt this border to be inflexible or too permeable—due to lack of validation and faulty barriers (either too rigid with deprivation and negative judgments, or too open with suffocating infantilizations)—suffers a lack of capacity to define inside and outside and a lack of capacity to flow across—outward and back. Sometimes this is felt only as a sense of confusion. A woman presented her dream and comments during a period when she felt she was leaving the safety of what she called her "father's definition system": "I dream I look through a glass wall and see a woman outside. She is in bed, dressed or under a snakeskin. What is inside? What outside? What is real? I feel as if my whole life is falling apart." But she was willing to dare the confusion. Another woman tried desperately to maintain control over her disorientation by holding inside and outside rigidly separate. She said, "There are two ways to relate—to other people out there and what they expect of me, and to myself, innerly. But that's so hidden and unfocused, it feels autistic. There I'm a lonely little princess, but I know no one could stand me." Both women had experienced a painful sense of discrepancy between outer collective and superego ideals and the perception of their own reality, which was hidden away because it was so much at variance with what "outside" would accept.

The transference-countertransference relationship, by reconstellating the parent-child container and the archaic-magic levels of consciousness, can permit experiences to heal those pathologies of the border. Empathy with its validating acceptance is the feeling mode that dissolves the overly rigid defensive border, and nurtures the uncontained confusion when there is no permeable resonance yet formed.

Enki as Patron of Therapists

Enki's wisdom can meet the dark primal goddess in the consciousness of her suffering, in the suffering of her becoming aware of her outside and inside—of herself.

For me, Enki is also the god of therapists. He is able to accomplish a basic restructuring of psychic inertia by using whatever is at hand—hidden under the fingernail. He moves the situation to a different perspective. He improvises. In this myth he brings in a previously irrelevant factor—a feeling for the plight of the goddess Inanna that extends to her underworld sister, a feeling that reverences the cause of stuckness itself. Instead of polarizing against the deep feminine power that the upper world fears because it seems only to end and fix life, he finds value where there seemed to be only misery. Enough value to affirm the goddess as misery and to mirror inside and outside pain—to give her that gift.

We do that when we turn towards an affect and intensify it to find its own vectors; or when we turn towards a defense and see it as having been life-preserving. We can even do it when we see pain as a valid part of life's process—no one's fault, just a fact of existence. This takes it out of the patriarchal-adversary-scapegoating perspective that blames someone or something and wants it removed, wants something actively done with it. Seeing pain as a part of the process enlarges the perspective that sees it only as a sign of pathology and a stigma. It permits empathy with the suffering and permits natural healing. It permits suffering through to gestate a new solution in its own way and its own time. Healing occurs then not only because the meaning or image is found, but because the process of life is given attention and empathetic presence and a mirroring that touches it wherever it is.

As therapists we are like those little, nonoppositional yin creatures, servants of the god Enki, in our work at this level of the psyche. We are present and accepting and letting be, expressing the truth of the dark affects. Such presence implies our trusting the *participation mystique* of the deepest layers of consciousness as a process of the goddess, sometimes even when it feels painful and seems to aim towards death and depression, and makes us feel keenly our own inadequacy to bring about change. There we wait with patience, going deeper and waiting together until the goddess as Time is ready to "decree a kind fate."

Working with this modality often requires the therapist to be willing to move in as close as the mourners, to be willing to share, with feeling, the pain of the complex constellated first in the patient. It implies the possibility of psychic infection and the sharing of the complex itself. From such a mutuality can emerge that radical healing which only occurs where a complex is shared—where both patient and therapist have gone down until they came to a shared woe. Then healing is often accomplished when the therapist works on his or her own experience of and attitude to the complex, or it may come about for both parties through a shift in the patient's psyche. There is so little clear differentiation; we can only say the mutually constellated field activates primal energies that spur the healing process.[131]

Such sharing—as one modality of therapy—affirms human life even in the darkness of misery. But sometimes in archaic phases of the negative transference, it means accepting the role of witness to the patient's onslaught against life, staying motionless except in sympathy. It means being willing to avoid taking away the force of the despair and rage with protestations defending our own ego stance, even expressing our own hurt, but staying with the patient who is caught and blind as meat in Ereshkigal's grip; feeling the pain and reverencing with echoing, participatory acceptance, not hurrying through the darkest pits of nature that feel slow with an abysmal, peristaltic rhythm at such times. When the transference container is strong and when there is enough consciousness to begin to feel the difference between self and other, then confrontation and interpretation are vital. But only after the container of acceptance has been established, a container in which the components of the personality can be congregated and within which the hidden seed of wholeness can grow.

Such empathy is unmanly to the heroic ego ideal. But there have always been taboos against going into the underworld proud, active, and emotionally vibrant. Gilgamesh advised Enkidu to travel there like a captive, or invisible. And the spiritual initiates to the "dark path of Persephone" and "grove of adored Aphrodite" are told to "put off their garments and all become . . . bridegrooms, 'robbed of their virility by the virgin spirit.'"[132] So therapists who work with the unconscious must be willing to endure personal invisibility and inaction. The mourners already have this necessary attitude. They were created yin, receptive. And having no defensive and adversary needs of their own, they can handle the raw stuff of the unconscious by echoing it back, witnessing. As Jung has written, handling allows us to find value and to humanize what is otherwise too stark and overpowering for the innocent or uninitiated participant:

> When these things appear out of the natural mind, they are horrible, even insupportable, but one discovers, when one handles them for awhile, that they are really exceedingly precious.[133]

*

Enki's asexual figures were created without specific gender. They are not eunuchs nor homoerotic. Yet they suggest the level of pregenital, polymorphous sexuality that serves the Great Goddess at this deep level of the psyche. Their image amplifies the frequent heroine or puella connection to men caught in service to the Great Mother through their artistic creativity or through their addictions or homosexuality. Because such a woman's own relation to her mother is poor, and because she cannot value her own sex or herself, she often seems to seek the feminine through the goddess' devoted son-lovers—men with whom she feels safe from genital and emotional penetration, men who offer passion and receptive sensitivity and their own resistance to the patriarchate. Similarly, homosexual men are often drawn to the Great Father behind the eternal father's daughter.

One woman's dream imaged her nascent sense of the goddess behind her homosexual partners:

> Two men who love each other are sitting in my kitchen. One is wounded. His penis was cut off. I kiss him and see that he slowly changes into a woman with large breasts. The other man kneels as the sex change proceeds quietly. The first man is now a woman. She reminds me of an ad I saw in the drug store for ageless skin—a beautiful, dark lady.

The kneeling man she associated to her father's brother, an artist and the shadow aspect of her father. But the woman feared to claim her Self's lonely authority because it seemed to endanger her relationships—bitter, tumultuous, and superficial as they were. Instead she depended on icy and intellectual maliciousness—the pretense of power she associated with the wounded, mother-dominated, homosexual male companion in the dream. The dream action images her turning towards this mode with an accepting kiss. She could begin to see its value as the only kind of assertion she had found. The kiss transforms the castrated homoerotic animus into an ageless, albeit collectively advertised, image of the goddess. And it permits her a direct, reverential relationship to the archetypal feminine.

Ereshkigal's Generosity

In the Ishtar versions of the Descent poems, Enki's way of approaching the feminine permits Ereshkigal to produce her essence, the water of life, which she holds in the underworld. It turns the cause of the inertia towards its own life-giving side. It stirs the tomb to bearing, shows us that the unconscious suffers and brings forth life.[134] Like the Gorgon whose blood kills or heals, Ereshkigal can destroy or create and heal —depending on what attitude we take to the dark goddess.

In the older versions of the myth Enki has provided his servants with the food and water of life from his own store.

And Ereshkigal, grateful for their reverent mirroring, turns towards them and appreciates their help and grants rewards. She offers the decree of "a kind fate," and "the water-gift, the river in its fullness," and "the grain-gift, the field in harvest." They ask for the corpse that hangs from the nail. Ereshkigal, all-knowing, names it, "the corpse of your mistress." And she gives it to them. She is beneficent, transformed, generous. A miracle has occurred through Inanna's sacrifice and Enki's finding of the right attitude. The fertility of the bull of heaven that had died is reborn in the dark womb.

The same motif appears in fairy tales, where for instance Baba Yaga and Mother Hulda grant their kindly faces when served with tact and submissive obedience by the women who visit them. And just so did a modern woman dream:

> I find a terrible, black-robed, black-faced woman standing near the window of the room overlooking the piazza. She turns to me and I feel a great fear. She tells me to go to the chapel and gather the old discarded grain stalks strewn on its floor, and to use the grain to bake her a loaf of bread. I am to find knife and mortar and pan in the corners of her dark room. With great difficulty, for I have never done this before, and very slowly, I manage to grind the flour. I have to use my own saliva to wet it. Finally I form a loaf and wonder where to bake it. The dark woman opens her skirts and shows me a glowing oven. I put the loaf into it, filled with awe. When I look up from my kneeling position, I see that her face is now luminous and kindly. I have never been so shaken with wonder.

To the goddess it is no shame for a woman to be submissive. But as von Franz has pointed out, such willing service is not always the way to gain what is necessary from the goddess of nature. Sometimes she must be approached with active, heroic courage rather than heroic submission. Gretel had to push the dark goddess into the oven of transformation. Sometimes she must be endured or avoided or cleverly fled from. It seems to depend on the conscious personality of the visitor and what qualities are to be gained from the dark side of the instinct and image pattern. For the high goddess Inanna, proud and passionate and active, submissive sacrifice, humility, and passive mirroring are the compensatory ways to set her free.

IX Returning and Its Price: The Scapegoat-Beloved

The Return of Inanna—Return of the Repressed

Often when the moment of return comes, we do not even know it. We may simply feel befuddled and dizzy like an infant, new before life. And so Inanna is revived. She is "sprinkled" with the food and water of life.[135] There is an anointing or libation of the oral, good stuff, a granting of value and validation in sprinkled doses. For just as initiates are often fed as if they were infants, so Inanna, the reborn initiate to the dark goddess, is sprinkled and returns to life slowly. The food and water represent new libido to replenish that lost in her sacrifice. They restore the soul's balance and permit Inanna to live again in the upper world.

In analysis we see this feeding in the necessity to offer validation over and over to the untrusting analysand in small, immunizing doses, until she or he can bear the experience of acceptance. It means guarding against haste, staying with the endless affects and events of daily life in all their detail until the flow of life energies returns to the stricken soul.

Inanna is restored to active life and rises from the underworld reborn. But she returns demonic, surrounded by the pitiless small demons of Ereshkigal, whose duty it is to claim the dead. In the myth they are to claim the underworld's substitute, and Inanna returns with "the eye of death" herself to choose her own scapegoat. She has met Ereshkigal and knows the abysmal reality: that all changes and life demand sacrifice. That is exactly the knowledge that patriarchal morality and the fathers' eternally maiden daughters have fled from, wanting to do things right in order to avoid the pain of bearing their own renewal, their own separate being and uniqueness. Inanna comes up loathesome and claiming her right to survive. She is not a beautiful maid, daughter of the fathers, but ugly, selfish, ruthless, willing to be very negative, willing not to care.

We know this demonic return of the repressed power shadow. Although it stands ultimately for life, it often erupts in birth and takes a lot of taming. It may be a "rough beast,"

78

or it may, indeed, merely feel fearsome when a woman comes out of hiding to stand her ground—to herself and/or to those around her. We see this demonic form of the returning goddess in much of the early women's liberation fury. For the most part that stage in the movement has passed, but each individual woman initiate may have to go through it.[136] At such a point in therapy a woman dreamt:

> I pay back what I owe to a man (who hides his passion under a sophisticated, intellectual façade). Suddenly all the sirens in the city go off, as if there is to be a nuclear attack. I realize there is no place to hide.

She described a nuclear attack as a cold, impersonal, destructive power.

Another woman feared to turn into a raging leopard if she asserted herself. But she also gloried in her power. "I can stand up to my husband now. I see I even want to wound him, not just let him hurt me. Let him come to terms with that," she threatened, relishing her newly claimed potency. It meant that her old sentimental and compliant containment in her marriage was no longer viable. She could no longer find indirect validation by playing fragile and all-accepting martyr. The old basis of the marriage relationship—pity and care-taking as a substitute for love between equals—had died, and both partners were forced to create a new relationship pattern between them. Thus individual change forges the new institutions of the post-patriarchal age.

The Scapegoat-Substitute Sacrifice

The problem for Inanna on her return is the substitute for herself. Whom can she choose as her scapegoat? The law of the conservation and sacrifice of energy permitted her release. In the myth this law is revealed to be the foundation of the year-god rites. As we have seen, only by sacrifice can the rupture of the wholeness pattern be rebalanced.

On one level we can see that only her best beloved consort is equal to Inanna. Indeed, in a love song she fashioned for Dumuzi she tells him:

> You, beloved, man of my heart,
> You, I have brought about an evil fate for you . . .
> Your right hand you have placed on my vulva,

Your left stroked my head,
You have touched your mouth to mine,
You have pressed my lips to your head.
That is why you have been decreed an evil fate,
Thus is treated the "dragon" of women.... [137]

Dumuzi's love of the goddess had brought him prosperity and great joy. But he had dared intimacy, and that entails a price. In the later mysteries it is forbidden to look upon the goddess' face and live. No mortal can endure the awesome face of reality and survive unscathed. Dumuzi has done that and more. Thus he has already been made sacred—or "sacrificed." As an initiate, the goddess takes him in her underworld aspect. This is the esoteric and psychological mystery of his sacrifice. Inanna challenges her equal to make the same descent she endured—perhaps to claim the same strength and wisdom.

Being the beloved hurts the most because it means being known and knowing the other's complexes in their depth. There are inevitable moments of "evil fate" since the intimate one opens the deepest wounds, and lovers, thus, become enemies. And they are also beloved enemies, since the woundings create separations across which fresh passions leap. Often, when we are meant to develop psychologically, we find ourselves choosing an intimate who will rub our noses in our worst complexes for just that purpose.

Perhaps, indeed, we only bother to hurt when we hold the other as dear as the necessity of speaking our own truth—when there is a genuine (albeit sometimes feared) equality. In situations of intimacy where there is no felt equality, it is extremely difficult to speak with the objective vision of the dark goddess, for speaking objectively then threatens our view of loving based on child needs for parental comfort and security. So, too often, we pussyfoot around, cringe and protect ourselves and the other when she or he seems too weak to bear the facts without terrible retaliation.

When we depend on the other for our validation, we remain compliant or erupt only unconsciously. But being willing to send down Dumuzi means daring to stand for our own reality, means daring to aim where we know there is a complex—even if it sends the other into defensiveness so his or her ego is lost to us in the underworld. That is the extraverted, challenge-to-the-beloved side of the confrontation with Dumuzi. On the introverted side, it implies that the ideal most cherished must be sacrificed, given up to the goddess. The beautiful agreeableness of the love goddess and the human father's daughter, the identification with spirit and with having things easy and innocent—those animus ideals must be redirected towards the dark goddess herself and changed profoundly in her service, in order that the woman as herself, in service to her Self, may survive. The beloved Dumuzi here is the favorite animus attitude, the old king, that the feminine soul must render to the Self, kill as the primary source of her own validation and identity.

Dumuzi

Mythologically, Dumuzi is the dying shepherd king, a prefiguration of Abel and Christ. His name means "faithful son"; his mother is, among shepherds, the goddess personifying the ewe, and among cowherders, the lady of wild cows. At other times his mother is said to be the reed goddess. (At no point is he a son of Inanna.) Dumuzi's father is Enki, the fertilizing waters upon which the harvest depends.[138] One form of Dumuzi is related to the god of the date palm, another to the grain and the power in the barley to produce beer.[139] Jacobsen calls him "the élan vital of new life in nature, vegetable and animal."[140]

But he is also the mortal king and shepherd of the people, a man identified with the principle of immortality as both the impregnator and the harvest of the land. On the Uruk vase of the fourth millenium he is depicted in his role as consort to Inanna in the sacred marriage rite. In this role he represents the fully incarnated man, but a kind of god-man, a man made immortal. As consort he is initiated into service to the immortal goddess of life and fertility. His consciousness is reconciled to life's limits, for it transcends them through the influx of transpersonal energy that gives him a sense of being that is embedded in resources beyond mortal powers. Like Apuleius who was made sunlike in his identification with the god and worshipped thus, so Dumuzi in his role of king and consort is deified.

But he is the mortal husband of the goddess of the land,

and he must die in order for earth's creation to renew itself. His human libido is needed to claim the all-giving earth, Inanna's breast, and to plow the soil, Inanna's vulva,[141] that she may bring fertility to the land. But his death is also necessary for renewal because, as king, he is identified with the harvests and the peak of divine perfection and force that inevitably fades. Here it is sacrificed in its prime, to move the cycle of living and dying seasons, of loving unions and painful separations, mergings and partings.

Before Inanna comes to the city of Erech and finds Dumuzi, there are three other figures who appear to her on her return—all of them dressed in sackcloth, throwing themselves at the feet of "mother" Inanna. Ninshubur and her own two sons, she spares from the demons. But Dumuzi she finds unconcerned for her plight. He is "dressed in noble garments ...sitting on a lofty throne."[142] He does not grovel at the sight of the goddess surrounded by demons. He does not descend from his throne. As consort and year god, he has been spared the pains of the barren land. He seems unconscious of the goddess except in her fertility and Aphroditic aspects, and he basks in his role as favorite—godlike and regal in his ignorance. On him Inanna vents her hatred and vengeance—the demonism of the returned goddess. On him she "fastened the eye of death, spoke the word against him, the word of wrath. ... "[143] In the world of light she repeats the actions of her dark sister, fully embodying in herself the underworld, death-dealing aspect of the goddess.

Until this moment Dumuzi is neither afraid nor servile. He is secure, identified with the god. He is strong enough—or sufficiently unconscious of his human frailty—to stand as favored consort and king, to stand as a god-man, not as child begging for pity from the mother. That means deeply honoring Inanna; for against Dumuzi she can own—and then tame in its own time—her deep need to survive. He meets her reality with his own separate and secure reality. He faces her down as equal, does not placate. So she does not have to care. She can cut through the unequal goddess-mortal, queen-servant, parent-child bondings; she can find the space in which to test him and to embody more of herself in the conscious world. From him she gains the profound respect of confrontation.

This suggests one of the ways in which transpersonal energies need a human partner—here not as a mirroring voice but as an equal dignity. Because Dumuzi had been identified with the goddess' consort, he could temporarily embody a transpersonal force to balance her own. Thus the onslaught of her demonic return is ended. The demons have a focus and can spend their fury in pursuit of Dumuzi. His capacity to confront them relieves the people of the land, for he stands as their champion and king, himself receiving the brunt of the fury, himself their scapegoat, their peace offering.

Often enough, in the modern world, a close family member or a therapist is chosen to bear the eruption of untamed energies when an initiate returns reborn, and initially demonic, from the underworld. If this can be acknowledged consciously and acquiesced in, it can be borne as part of the overall process.

This part of the myth points up the psychological problems of women identified with the culture's perverted ideal of mushy, self-abnegating relatedness as a means of gaining validation. They let their own needs be turned aside when they are seen as motherly or commiserated with. They lose true relatedness to allow themselves to merge, but such merging is simply a way of avoiding confrontation. It keeps a woman's strength, which she needs to foster her individual integrity, in the underworld. But the complex of individual identity does not lose its energy. The strength in it refluxes, and the woman goes back into depression in a recurrent cycle. Or it seeks on until it finds someone who can adequately meet it, who can stand and receive the passionate energy of the complex and ground it—by feeling respect for the energy itself and the woman's necessity to embody it.

Through seeing the pain inflicted, the passionate one may let herself be transformed by grief and remorse. But too often a woman's strength is turned aside prematurely by father or husband or brother, so caught in his own mother complex that he cannot stand firm. Then he grovels and placates like Inanna's sons, or furies like a bull in hell out of his own unconscious depths. And the woman's assertive energy, with which she might claim her separate, individual identity is turned back on itself and her own physical and psychological children, or it moves into passive-aggressive manoeuvres. In either case she loses another chance to validate her own necessity. Here women need help from each other and from men, for we are just learning our independence from old, sentimental ideals, and we can be obnoxious as we learn to assume our full identities.

In this context Dumuzi's lack of reverence for the reborn Inanna can be seen from a different perspective, one which is too often relevant in the present time as women struggle to bring their strengths and sufferings into consciousness. Dumuzi has celebrated while his partner suffered. He does not value her descent and ignores her return, for he may be seen to have a very poor relationship to his own vulnerable sensitivity and depths. Thus he negates the goddess, hides from her pain and need by being grandiose and blithe. Unlike the "sons" who are overawed and too abject, he is too high, lacking all empathic concern for Inanna.

We see this often enough in the reactions of the narcissistic man who negates or belittles his partner's pain—after she has given birth or when she is in anguish about finding her own independent stance outside "his" family. The man may then play "poor-me" or "royal me-first," subtly or overtly undermining a woman's struggle. Especially when she begins to find her strength and to challenge his previously assumed primacy, he may try to wriggle out of his responsibility by blaming or derogating her, or by taking flight in passivity or aloofness. Thus be betrays his need to descend into the underworld himself, his need to find a relationship to an inner feminine whom he can accept nondefensively and revere as equal.

In the myth Dumuzi's transmutation into a snake could be taken symbolically as one way in which he tries to wriggle out of his own necessity to confront the depths of the unconscious. His flight to his sister, as the lysis of another poem, provides a more hopeful prognosis regarding his individuality and anima development.

X   Balancing: The Acceptance of Process

One Lysis: The Wisdom of Change

"Take him away," Inanna decrees. And the demons, instruments of fate "who accept no gifts," bind and beat Dumuzi. His experience of torture is not unlike that of Job's and of Christ's agony. And like his mythological descendants he appeals to god to spare him. For through suffering Dumuzi awakens fully to the reverence of fear and to his mortality. He is wrenched from his regal, godlike state and made suddenly aware of time's limit and of human insecurity and death. Confronting the dark aspect of the goddess Inanna, he feels fear and pain. And these teach him awe of the goddess and the value of his mortal life. He tries to save himself. He offers his tears. He appeals to Utu, the solar god, who arranged his marriage to Inanna. He asks to be transformed into a snake. And Utu hears him.

Unlike Gilgamesh, Dumuzi does not lose his immortality to the serpent. Instead, by being transformed into a snake, Dumuzi gains the serpent wisdom: that nothing in the Great Round dies. Like the snake that sheds its skin (as Inanna shed her regalia), life's forms are lost and renewed. The undying energy of the serpent-power remains. So Dumuzi in other incarnations will climb upon Inanna's throne and bed serving as mortal consort of the immortal goddess of life. The institution of divine kingship, symbol of renewed life, will continue, and through it Dumuzi will "escape" his mortality. This poem ends with the words that as a snake, "Dumuzi, the king, escaped from his demons."[144] This is the "escape" of the initiate and of the magic-matriarchal dimension of consciousness, a perspective of the wholeness pattern of the energy transformation cycle.

The transformation is here provided by Utu, the solar brother of Inanna. In response to Dumuzi's tears, his offering of mortal pain and terror, Utu makes Dumuzi sacred. He sacrifices his human incarnation and grants him the undying form of the snake, immortal consort of the goddess, symbol of the energy of life.

Utu, the sun god, is the balance of Ereshkigal. He—like Enki—is outside the patriarchal Logos modes, not adversary but complement of the feminine. Like other solar divinities he stands for the feminine as twin of the nocturnal moon or star goddess (or as son or consort of the earth). His message—through the transformation he works on Dumuzi—suggests that life continues, that there are no fixed limits, only transformations of energy. This balances Dumuzi's fear, just as Ereshkigal's message—life ends, there are limits and separations—balances Inanna's virgin innocence. The solar god and the dark goddess are the pillars of the esoteric temple with its wisdom of change. There is no lysis that we would find stable in this myth, no resolution except that profound wisdom.

Psychologically we often see such a shape-change when a person is gripped by terrible fear and an adversary that is too powerful. Fear then drives him or her out of the human dimension. One loses one's human soul like Dumuzi, whose "soul left him like a hawk flying against a bird."[145] The person falls into the unconscious, is overcome with emotion, gets panicky. In identity with the fear, one attempts to survive the onslaught. One seeks thus to hide out of life until there is opportunity to be reborn in a more clement environment. Fear engulfs the mortal soul and causes its descent. Then the underworld can be a place to hide, a refuge. We see this descent in negative animus and anima attacks, when emotionality overcomes one's sense of personal identity. We see it also in the life stories of individuals who feel outsiders and scapegoats, having found no adequate safety in any validating environment. Then the underworld is their soul's painful refuge, and their return to life often occurs in the pattern of Inanna's story.

Another Lysis: Inanna's Remorse and a Rebalance of Energy

In other myths—"The Most Bitter Cry,"[146] "Dumuzi's Dream," and "The Return"[147]—the story ends in different ways. Two new elements are added. There is Inanna's reaction to the death of her consort, and there is a new character, Dumuzi's sister Geshtinanna.

First, there are songs of the Great Goddess' grief over the loss of her beloved:

Inanna laments for her young bridegroom,
"Gone is my husband, sweet husband, ...
My husband has gone among the ... plants, ...
My husband who has gone to seek food, has been turned over
to the plants ...
...who has gone to seek water, had been turned over to the
water.
My bridegroom, like a hand crushed..., has departed from
the city.... "[148]

She weeps that he has been "taken captive," been "killed,"
"no longer bathes," "no longer treats the mother of Inanna as
his mother," "no longer competes with the lads of his city,"
"no longer performs his sweet task among the maidens of his
city." Inanna is bereft. She searches for her lost beloved. She
"sweetens the place where her husband lies," the desert steppe
that is his grave (outside the city, where later Hebraic scapegoats were taken), by transforming an old mother-of-sons goddess into a waterskin so that the travelling lad will have fresh
water to drink there. This suggests the transformation of an
old source and containment of libido into a new one. The
traveller to the underworld will thus know that he is loved,
and be able to drink from that maternal font even in his
desert and desolate wanderings. That is a great comfort of the
goddess and suggests that maternal sustenance can change its
form to freshen even our descents into what feels like death.

The goddess mourns her beloved. Even she cannot escape
the profound sadness in the feeling heart that change incurs.
As instrument of fate, she causes the sadness; but she also
suffers it and relieves it. In the underworld she was unconscious of her own transformation while Ereshkigal groaned. In
the Great Above Inanna suffers the separation from her beloved.

But there are other songs throughout the dynasties of
Sumer describing her joyful reunitings with Dumuzi in his
renewed incarnations as king of her land and city. "On the
day of 'sleeping,'/On the New Year, the day of rites," she
takes others to her bed in the sacred marriage rite. And the
cycle of undying life is celebrated.[149]

The Great Goddess rejoices and mourns as her own process, of life-death change through time, brings her new mor-
tals and takes them away in an eternal round of consorts—

until Gilgamesh defies his role, spurns her offer of the sacred marriage, puts the institution of kingship on a new basis, and upholds the derogation of the goddess. Inanna, like Ereshkigal, is an archetypal energy pattern. Each generation of humans is altered and affected by contact with the enduring bipolar goddess, and needs to find and create life-sustaining balances within their grand pattern. For humans must ever shift, struggling and flowing, to stay in equilibrium—including enough of Ninshubur's realism and service to survive in the mundane world. It is a never-ending play, a balancing act, without a fixed or even ideal end.

A Third Lysis: Geshtinanna, Dumuzi's Sister

But the problem is even more complicated when seen from the human perspective. The goddess Inanna, for all her archetypal intensity, lacks our capacity for personal human connection. She is served by any mortal in the role of Dumuzi. She is the goddess, unrelated except to her own inherent necessities and to the other impersonal intensities. We humans have a harder problem, for we are also, being small and time-space bound, embedded in a network of personal intimacies.

We serve and are patterned and fueled by the archetypal energies, the goddesses, but also we care about ourselves embodied on earth and about the other fragile creatures with whom we share our destinies. Not only do we struggle to stay in conscious relation to the archetypal realm, and yet to avoid identification with any particular archetype in order to keep the balance fluid and life enhancing; yet must we also stand for Inanna as goddess of passions and affects, of love and war, as goddess supporting our personal, time-bound life on earth. We must also serve her by sustaining the earthly and human realm and its embodied necessities. For we find the goddess in and through our personal connections, incarnated in the place where we suffer our passions: in daily life. And this, as the myth of "Dumuzi's Dream" suggests (see below), also serves Inanna, the great, impersonal goddess. For through our passions and sacrifices, the goddess is given back her beloved, and life can flow forth from her holy womb.

The very nature of earth's life, and of the goddess herself, prevents the possibility of her having an undying, single partner. The goddess' fructifying consort is mortal, a god-man, a man made god in his service to her. He embodies the life-death bipolarity of the eternal process of change. That frightens and disgusts the side of us that, like Gilgamesh, wants eternity and stasis. But as the goddess is also matter, there is no stasis and no eternity of form possible for material life. We must gain our eternity in another way, not by clinging to the embodied identities we call heroic ideals. We must go beyond Gilgamesh's and the patriarchal ego's denigration of the goddess as fickle and learn to serve her rather as inconstant. This is the primary psychological task to which our age is called.

In the myth of "Dumuzi's Dream" we are pointed in this direction by a new character introduced into the myths. The shepherd king's sister, Geshtinanna, brings us out of the dramatic intensity of the sweeping mythic forces. She bridges the vivid, overwhelming energy patterns laid forth in the Inanna material, and the patterns of the smaller, earthly, human, personal world. She points us to a possibility of keeping our reverence for the goddess of life and eath, beyond the patriarchy. But at a price: the price of willing *acceptance*.

*

Geshtinanna, Dumuzi's sister, daughter of Enki and his wife, the reed goddess, is a wise woman, "a tablet-knowing scribe ...who knows the meaning of words,...who knows the meaning of dreams."[150] In the poem, the shepherd has a dream imaging the destruction of his work and himself. He sees a single reed bowed in mourning, and two reeds cut down. He calls upon his sister to interpret his vision. She sees it as foretelling their mother's mourning and his fated destiny and her own. She urges her brother to flee. She sees "the demons coming against" him, and vows to protect him with her silence even when she is tortured on his behalf. Later when he flees to her house and is seized for the last time, she laments wildly and searches for her brother.

Like Ninshubur, but in service to the human dimension, Geshtinanna does what she can to redeem the one lost to the underworld. She follows the destiny she saw in Dumuzi's dream. But she does it as a mortal woman and she does it through the goddess, not through the high gods. With Inanna, whose friend she is in other myths and whose love for Dumuzi she well knows,[151] she finds Dumuzi's grave and grieves. Then with full consciousness—and following the pattern established by the goddess—she offers to take her brother's place in the underworld. She acquiesces to her own cutting down.

Both she and Inanna descend after they suffer a separation and loss: the death of a vital partner. (Thus graves have always been considered entrances to the underworld and its unconscious depths.) But Geshtinanna offers herself not out of the goddess' love of adventure and strength. Her motivation is human passion—love and grief. And Inanna is so moved by her offer of sacrifice that she transmutes Dumuzi's sentence, and she mitigates the destiny laid out for Geshtinanna in the dream. She decrees that brother and sister shall alternate, each spending six months in the underworld and six months on earth. The goddess allows them to embody the process of her own cycle—descent and return, return and descent—the endless rearrangements of life's pattern.

The name Geshtinanna means "vine of heaven." One of her epithets is "root stock of the grapevine."[152] She is the force of the autumn-harvested grape and of its spring-fermented wine, just as Dumuzi personifies spring-harvested grain and its fermented beer. She is as close to her brother as Inanna is to Utu, the sun god. Perhaps even closer, for there is a poem in which the shepherd introduces Geshtinanna to sexuality, showing her incest among the animals of his sheepfold. She stands as earthly, "rooted-stock," sister of the gemini pair. She has to do with endogamous libido in kinship that is an intimate, personal connection to the masculine, born together out of the same womb and dying together, the two cut down in the same image. Thus Geshtinanna personifies the woman who can be sister-comrade to mortal man. She is caring in a way that goes beyond the goddess' impersonal capacity, seeing life's fragile patterns in her human wisdom, willing to share their burden in her human grief and love; she serves the reborn goddess, but can have her own standpoint as well.

Geshtinanna comes into the story after Inanna's descent and return. She does not feel the defensiveness of a daughter of the fathers for whom any self-sacrifice for the masculine—without seeking payment for herself in returned gratification—is very hard. Her capacity for relatedness goes closer, is more specific and embodied in earthly feeling—beyond the goddess' impersonal, queenly rhythms and primal affects. She can read the messages of the unconscious, yet she can stand firm even against demons. She is an image for one who can mediate between the human and transpersonal realms and share the burden of weaving them together.

Geshtinanna seems to symbolize the product of Inanna's descent and return: a budded offshoot of the goddess' encounter with her own dark sister, a new "root stock of the vine" of life. Yet, compared to the Great Goddess, she seems humble and human and humanly conscious. As daughter of Enki, she is supportive of the feeling dimension. She shelters her brother in his fear and dependency, and she responds creatively to his destiny, for she is close kin to his fate and feelings. Unlike the god-man consort, she is "a wise woman." She is conscious. She has been made conscious by both his fear and by the dream. But she is strong enough to mitigate and to take upon herself human suffering, through conscious, loving sacrifice. She offers herself to the goddess, her friend, out of passionate love for her human brother. Thus she does not flee from her fate, nor does she denigrate the goddess of fate as do Gilgamesh and the patriarchy. She volunteers. And in this courageous, conscious acquiescing, she ends the pattern of scapegoating by choosing to confront the underworld herself. Willingly, she offers to serve Ereshkigal as well as Inanna.

Her image is Christlike, yet more personal than Christ's, and deeply feminine. He gave his life for all men, a grand gesture. She offers herself, courageously accepting her own destiny, for one man she cares for, her brother, whom she calls "beloved man."[153] It is a small, personal answer, an individual and individualized response; it is her own creative act to serve Inanna's process of life and her own incarnated constellation of the goddess of love and war—her own personal feelings. On this earth that is the limit of our experienced feeling: specific, here-and-now evaluation. We may extrapolate from it, but that is the scale on which we experience it.

Geshtinanna is not a grand model, a single answer to the process. She is herself, and her response is specific to her own feelings and her own fulfillment. She simply shows us the problems and her own resolution. But, for me, she conveys the possibility of an incarnated capacity to serve both the goddess and human life. She is a result of, and an embodiment of, the whole initiation process—the creation of Inanna's renewed darkness and passion and remorse, and of Dumuzi's divine kingship and human dependency and fear. She feels personally and can be lovingly related as partner of the masculine. She is also willing to serve both the light and dark aspects of her own depths and of the goddess. As she is portrayed in the poems, she lacks the vibrancy of Inanna. She also does not yet know Ereshkigal's domain, for she has not yet made her own descent. There is no struggle in her character between her instinct to relate to her beloved and her instinct to stand alone and for her own depths. But she is willing to dare the descent. And that is what many modern women are called upon by their dreams and feelings to do.

As the poem ends Geshtinanna has not yet gone down. Dumuzi goes first. This suggests that animus or superego ideals must be overcome before a woman can make her own direct, individual descent.

We can wonder what will change in Geshtinanna, how she will be different on her first return and on all the subsequent ones. For each descent is a new process, and she may return with different balance each time. We can wonder how any human woman or anima is to be transformed through our rhythm of service to Inanna and the world of the Great Above —with its active passions, extraverted and collective relationships, and creative expression—and to Ereshkigal and the world of incubating dark and seeming stasis, where the collective unconscious works upon us and we come to our aloneness rooted in the goddess and *muladhara*. It is for us to endure the phases of descent-ascent-descent, as a service to both aspects of the feminine instinct and spirit patterns. It is hard to say and feel "Holy Ereshkigal, sweet is your praise!" Yet that is as essential as our welcoming back the full range of the feminine, symbolized by Inanna, to the above, conscious world. Acknowledging Ereshkigal can lead us to find meaning in pain and loss and even in death, just as we need to reaffirm the meaning in Inanna's passionate joy and combat and ambition —all valid and holy experiences for women.

Embodying the process—with her brother-animus, alternating in the above and below, enduring and embracing the play of opposites—Geshtinanna stands outside the patriarchal mode, for her stance is ever creative, ever relative and flexible. It cannot be reached deliberately as an ideal—only by suffering the individualized feelings and passions that in her represent her service to the goddess, and by enduring the descents and returns demanded by the goddess. As wine she symbolizes a new feminine spirit and an old, yet ever-new, consciousness of process. Every new crop of the vine must descend for fermentation into the underworld and come up transformed as the fruit also of underworld transformation. As the ever-new wine, taste and quality will vary; each year's crop will be different from another's. There is no abstract standard of perfection that can—or even needs to be—attained. It is a process of earth's organic rhythms, which is why the taste and quality must vary. And that is the point—part of feeling-discrimination and its joy and sorrow.

Forerunner of Dionysus, Geshtinanna points us towards a new kind of individuating ego: one that celebrates and acquiesces in the transformation processes of life and death; one that embodies an ever-changing balance between transpersonal and personal;[154] one that dares to encounter the shadows in the underworld and to return to life feelingly and humanly embodying, not repressing, their energies.

There are problems with the facts of Geshtinanna's fate as a paradigm for modern women. Her fate—as decreed by the goddess—can give us faith in the process of change, which is a help in letting go consciously and being willing to live into new psychological spaces. And like many of us, she chooses to serve her own individual destiny—but as that was conceived in ancient Sumer.

We would probably not long be able to accept a fate that prevented our living out a more conscious relation to the partner (or animus). Sumer solved the problems of relationship by positing an alternation of conscious and unconscious positions: Geshtinanna and Dumuzi do not again meet; they pass twice a year in the endless cycle. And we get no hint of psychological development, of the accretion of wisdom as the years turn.

We modern women have a long history that is becoming more and more conscious. We can feel the effects of our lay struggles in the patriarchy and in the underworld. And we must, as Jung put it, "dream the myth on." There are no paradigms that exactly fit our situation. We can only know from this ancient tale what forces we must serve. How each of us is to find our own individual balance and development as we descend-ascend and ascend-descend—that is still to be lived and written.

Summary

The Inanna mythologems of descent and return reintroduce two great goddesses, primal feminine energy patterns and their partners, and the possibility of an individual human response to bring them into incarnated, personal life. The story presents a model for health and for healing the split between above and below, between the collective ideal and the powerful bipolar, transformative, processual reality underlying the feminine wholeness pattern. The images of the myth can orient us on the path as we suffer the return to the goddess and renewal, following in the footsteps of Inanna— and then of Geshtinanna.

The implication for modern women is that only after the full, even demonic, range of affects and objectivity of the dark feminine is felt and claimed can a true, soul-met, passionate and individual comradeship be possible between woman and man as equals. Inanna is joined to and separated from her dark ancestress-sister, the repressed feminine. And that, with Ninshubur's and Enki's and Dumuzi's help, brings forth Geshtinanna—a model of one who can take her stand, hold her own value, and be lovingly related to the masculine as well as directly to her own depths; a model of one who is willing to suffer humanly, personally, the full spectrum that is the goddess.

Glossary of Jungian Terms

Anima (Latin, "soul"). The unconscious, feminine side of a man's personality. She is personified in dreams by images of women ranging from prostitute and seductress to spiritual guide (Wisdom). She is the Eros principle, hence a man's anima development is reflected in how he relates to women. Identification with the anima can appear as moodiness, effeminacy, and oversensitivity.

Animus (Latin, "spirit"). The unconscious, masculine side of a woman's personality. He personifies the Logos principle. Identification with the animus can cause a woman to become rigid, opinionated, and argumentative. More positively, he is the inner man who acts as a bridge between the woman's ego and her own creative resources in the unconscious.

Archetypes. Irrepresentable in themselves, but their effects appear in consciousness as the archetypal images and ideas. These are collective universal patterns or motifs which come from the collective unconscious and are the basic content of religions, mythologies, legends, and fairytales. They emerge in individuals through dreams and visions.

Association. A spontaneous flow of interconnected thoughts and images around a specific idea, determined by unconscious connections.

Complex. An emotionally charged group of ideas or images. At the "center" of a complex is an archetype or archetypal image.

Constellate. Whenever there is a strong emotional reaction to a person or a situation, a complex has been constellated (activated).

Ego. The central complex in the field of consciousness. A strong ego can relate objectively to activated contents of the unconscious (i.e., other complexes), rather than identifying with them, which appears as a state of possession.

Feeling. One of the four psychic functions. It is a rational function which evaluates the worth of relationships and situations. Feeling must be distinguished from emotion, which is due to an activated complex.

Individuation. The conscious realization of one's unique psychological reality, including both strengths and limitations. It leads to the experience of the Self as the regulating center of the psyche.

Inflation. A state in which one has an unrealistically high or low (negative inflation) sense of identity. It indicates a regression of consciousness into unconsciousness, which typically happens when the ego takes too many unconscious contents upon itself and loses the faculty of discrimination.

95

Intuition. One of the four psychic functions. It is the irrational function which tells us the possibilities inherent in the present. In contrast to sensation (the function which perceives immediate reality through the physical senses) intuition perceives via the unconscious, e.g., flashes of insight of unknown origin.

Participation mystique. A term derived from the anthropologist Lévy-Bruhl, denoting a primitive, psychological connection with objects, or between persons, resulting in a strong unconscious bond.

Persona (Latin, "actor's mask"). One's social role, derived from the expectations of society and early training. A strong ego relates to the outside world through a flexible persona; identification with a specific persona (doctor, scholar, artist, etc.) inhibits psychological development.

Projection. The process whereby an unconscious quality or characteristic of one's own is perceived and reacted to in an outer object or person. Projection of the anima or animus onto a real woman or man is experienced as falling in love. Frustrated expectations indicate the need to withdraw projections, in order to be able to relate to the reality of other people.

Puella aeterna (Latin, "eternal girl"). Indicates a certain type of woman who remains too long in adolescent psychology, generally associated with a strong unconscious attachment to the father. Her male counterpart is the **puer aeternus,** an "eternal youth" with a corresponding tie to the mother.

Self. The archetype of wholeness and the regulating center of the personality. It is experienced as a transpersonal power which transcends the ego, e.g., God.

Shadow. An unconscious part of the personality characterized by traits and attitudes which the conscious ego tends to reject. It is personified in dreams by persons of the same sex as the dreamer.

Symbol. The best possible expression for something essentially unknown. Symbolic thinking is non-linear, right-brain oriented; it is complementary to logical, linear, left-brain thinking.

Transcendent function. The reconciling "third" which emerges from the unconscious (in the form of a symbol or a new attitude) after the conflicting opposites have been consciously differentiated, and the tension between them held.

Transference and counter-transference. Particular cases of projection, commonly used to describe the unconscious, emotional bonds that arise between two persons in an analytic or therapeutic relationship.

Uroborus. The mythical snake or dragon that eats its own tail. It is a symbol both for individuation as a self-contained, circular process, and for narcissistic self-absorption.

Notes

Refer to Bibliography for publication details not given here

1. Erich Neumann, "On the Moon and Matriarchal Consciousness," in *Fathers and Mothers,* p. 59.
2. Neumann, "Psychological Stages of Feminine Development," p. 96.
3. Adrienne Rich, "Reforming the Crystal," in *Poems: Selected and New, 1950-1974,* p. 228.
4. Carolyn G. Heilbrun, *Reinventing Womanhood,* pp. 37-50.
5. Samuel Noah Kramer, *The Sacred Marriage Rite: Aspects of Faith, Myth, and Ritual in Ancient Sumer,* pp. 108-121; and Diane Wolkstein and Samuel Noah Kramer, *Inanna, Queen of Heaven and Earth, Her Stories and Hymns.*
6. Alexander Heidel, *The Gilgamesh Epic and Old Testament Parallels,* pp. 119-128.
7. Thorkild Jacobsen, *The Treasures of Darkness: A History of Mesopotamian Religion,* p. 55.
8. Kramer, *Sacred Marriage Rite,* p. 108.
9. Ibid., p. 112.
10. Wolkstein and Kramer.
11. See, for example, Tillie Olsen, *Silences;* Adrienne Rich, *Of Woman Born* and *On Lies, Secrets, and Silences;* Carolyn Heilbrun, *Reinventing Womanhood;* and Dorothy Dinerstein, *The Mermaid and the Minotaur.* It is worth pointing out here that even Toni Wolff, in her essay "Structural Forms of the Feminine Psyche" (Zurich, 1946—available in most C.G. Jung Center Libraries), explains her categories—Mother, Amazon, Hetaera, Medial woman—primarily in relation to the masculine. Although valid, they need to be understood more introvertedly than she wrote about them, namely in terms of mothering, partnering, and mediating to our own feminine depths rather than just to outer, male partners.
12. See David R. Kingsley, *The Sword and the Flute;* and Beverley Zabriskie, "Isis, Ancient Goddess, Modern Woman."
13. Samuel Noah Kramer, *From the Poetry of Sumer,* pp. 27ff.
14. See Erich Neumann, *The Origins and History of Consciousness;* and Edward C. Whitmont, "The Momentum of Man."
15. "Inanna and the Huluppu Tree," in Wolkstein and Kramer.
16. Jacobsen, p. 623.

17. Heidel, p. 134.

18. Perhaps the soul is considered feminine because so much female body-ego experience entails boundary penetration from within and without (e.g., menstruation, sexual intercourse, childbirth, and lactation). This body experience prepares the ego for its capacity to be acted upon, to let another exert influence upon it. And this penetration is analogous to the soul's penetration by the divine. In many cultures the worshipper is likened to a bride or wife of the god. Men are enjoined to emulate Radha or Christ's bride, and to submit to the transpersonal godhead. Women have, also in many cultures, generally taken charge of daily eating and excretory functions for some others. There is an analogy between these "lowly" activities and the careful tending of the soul's reception of the numinous above and below.

19. Jean Gebser, "The Foundations of the Aperspective World."

20. C.G. Jung, "The Psychological Aspects of the Kore," in C.G. Jung and C. Kerényi, *Essays on a Science of Mythology*, p. 170.

21. Jacobsen suggests that the earliest form of her name was Ninanna(k), "Lady of the Date Cluster" (p. 36).

22. See Rodney Collin, *The Theory of Celestial Influence* (New York: Samuel Weiser Inc., 1954). The eight-year cycle of the planet Venus "appears to rule growth and the multiplication of mankind" (p. 298). Studies have shown that the planet's periodicity correlates with major crop yield (p. 276).

23. Kramer, *Poetry of Sumer*, p. 94.

24. For his human, heroic help, Gilgamesh received reward of the *pukku* and *mikku*, royal emblems that later fell into the underworld and brought about his knowledge of mortality. (See the Introduction to Wolkstein and Kramer for a fuller discussion of this story, "Inanna and the Huluppu Tree.")

25. Jacobsen, p. 137.

26. Kramer, *Poetry of Sumer*, p. 88.

27. Ibid., p. 97.

28. Jacobsen, p. 138.

29. Kramer, *Sacred Marriage Rite*, p. 96.

30. Ibid., p. 59.

31. Jacobsen, p. 141.

32. Karl Kerényi, *Athene: Virgin and Mother*, p. 45.

33. Kerényi, "Kore," in Jung and Kerényi, *Science of Mythology*, p. 105.

34. Inanna describes her two sons: one "who sings hymns to me/ Who cuts my nails and smooths my hair," and one who "is my right arm./He is my left arm./He is my leader" (Wolkstein and Kramer, pp. 66, 67). They are not lovers. And she makes sure they are not destroyed by the demons in the Descent poem. Her beloved consort is Dumuzi, who is not her son. And it is he whom she finally chooses to send as her substitute into the underworld. At a few points in the love poems she is made to refer to Dumuzi as "son" or "brother" (Kramer, *Sacred Marriage Rite*, pp. 96-97), but this seems merely a Sumerian use of the kinship words to indicate the quality of emotional closeness or respect. Such familial appelations are frequent in Sumer (and we know them too from tribal anthropology); thus also Inanna calls Ereshkigal "elder sister." Inanna is the earliest Great Goddess we know who sacrifices a lover in her stead. He is the year king. But the year king is not the son. He is the beloved mortal who has been made equal to the goddess (see below, chap. 9).

35. Heidel, pp. 50-52.

36. Kramer, *Poetry of Sumer,* p. 92.

37. Ezra 10:3-43.

38. See Michelle Zimbalist Rosaldo and Louise Lamphere, eds., *Woman, Culture, and Society.*

39. Edward C. Whitmont, work in progress.

40. *New York Times,* 12 August 1980, p. C7.

41. See C.G. Jung, "The Symbolic Life," in *Collected Works,* vol. 18, pars. 630ff.

42. Jacobsen, p. 99.

43. Samuel Noah Kramer, *Sumerian Mythology,* pp. 43-47.

44. Kerényi, "Kore," in Jung and Kerényi, *Science of Mythology,* p. 125.

45. "Inanna and the Huluppu Tree," in Wolkstein and Kramer.

46. So Jacobsen's translation of the above line is equally relevant: "Ereshkigal was given the *kur* as a prize." She became Queen. For with the separation of heaven and earth, the *kur* became her Great Dwelling and the place of a new fertility for her.

47. Similarly, the initiates into the Eleusinian Mysteries found comfort in Persephone-Demeter and the knowledge of eternal life gained through the mystery.

48. At times the moon god and Gilgamesh, and even the sun god and Dumuzi in his underworld form, join her judges (Jacobsen, p. 228).

49. Ibid.
50. Heidel, p. 122.
51. Kramer, *Sacred Marriage Rite*, p. 113.
52. Heidel, p. 122.
53. Kingsley, pp. 140-141.
54. Swami Rama et al., *Yoga and Psychotherapy: The Evolution of Consciousness*, pp. 226-231.
55. Kimberley McKell, *The Psychology of the Tantric Chakras.*
56. Marie-Louse von Franz, "The Handless Maiden," in *Problems of the Feminine in Fairytales*, pp. 70-78.
57. Depression is now two to six times more prevalent in women than in men in the United States. See Maggie Scarf, *Unfinished Business: Pressure Points in the Lives of Women* (New York: Doubleday, 1980) for a lay person's review of the subject.
58. Sylvia Perera Massell, "The Scapegoat Complex."
59. Patricia Berry, "The Rape of Demeter/Persephone and Neurosis."
60. Jane Ellen Harrison, *Prolegomena to the Study of Greek Religion*, pp. 8ff.
61. Enki taught them, thus, to stop one of Namtar's plagues (Jacobsen, p. 118).
62. Marie-Louise von Franz, *Shadow and Evil in Fairy Tales*, p. 167.
63. Heidel, p. 129.
64. Jacobsen, p. 229.
65. Dinerstein, *The Mermaid and the Minotaur.*
66. Edward C. Whitmont, "The Momentum of Man."
67. Kramer, *Sacred Marriage Rite*, p. 114.
68. C.G. Jung, "Psychological Commentary on Kundalini Yoga" (Lecture 1, Oct. 1932), in *Spring 1975*, p. 2.
69. Linda Fierz-David's words apply aptly to Inanna, although the word "merging" would be more appropriate in her text than "relatedness": "To live according to the principle of relatedness, to let oneself be entangled and to entangle others, is a necessity of nature for all women. . . . But as soon as the relatedness is carried on at the expense of one's own soul, as soon as the women flow over all too unreservedly into the world surrounding them . . . a powerful counter-current arises in them. . . . The spirit appears to them as death . . . over against overburdened life, *death* reveals itself to them *as the highest value.* . . . herald[ing] to them the frightful necessity of

rending all ties *in themselves* and giving up all relatedness in
the world, in order to find the relationship to the spirit and
therewith also to themselves.... They must... dare the leap
into darkness.... Women, in the cold breath of the spirit
realm, must experience also their own coldness.... [in order
to] deliver them from the compulsion of a relatedness that is
in thralldom to nature" ("Psychological Reflections on the
Fresco Series of the Villa of the Mysteries in Pompeii," pp.
93-97).

70. Von Franz, *Shadow and Evil*, p. 169.

71. Antonio T. de Nicolas, *Meditations through the Rig-Veda:
Four-Dimensional Man*, p. 24.

72. Joseph Campbell, *Myths to Live By*, pp. 103-104.

73. This is part of the teaching of the Bhagavad-Gita.

74. Kramer, *Sacred Marriage Rite*, p. 116.

75. Jacobsen, p. 58.

76. Kramer, *Sacred Marriage Rite*, p. 116.

77. Gertrude Ujhely, "Thoughts Concerning the *Causa Finalis* of
the Cognitive Mode Inherent in Pre-Oedipal Psychopathology." See also Dorothee Soelle, *Suffering*, trans. Everett R.
Kalen (Philadelphia: Fortress Press, 1975).

78. Penelope Washbourne, ed., *Seasons of Women*, p. 52.

79. Quoted by Margaret W. Masson in "The Typology of the
Female as a Model for the Regenerate: Puritan Preaching,
1690-1730," p. 312.

80. Gerard Manley Hopkins, *Poems and Prose of Gerard Manley
Hopkins,* ed. W.H. Gardner (London, 1953), p. 61.

81. Esther Harding, *Woman's Mysteries*, p. 84.

82. Ibid., pp. 135ff.

83. There is this capacity in men, of course, and sometimes animus figures in dreams image the more feminine yang. Both
are valid and necessary for both sexes.

84. T.-W. Danzell; quoted by Erich Neumann in *The Great
Mother*, p. 197.

85. This division of the two goddesses suggests an ancient, intuitive awareness of brain functioning only recently confirmed
scientifically by Paul MacLean and others. (See, for instance,
Mary Long, "Ritual and Deceit," in *Science Digest*, Nov/Dec
1980, pp. 87-121.) The primitive, "reptilian" brain is responsible for self-preservation, violent aggression, dominance, and
ritually repetitive display behaviors. These are roughly analogous to behavior patterns associated by the Sumerians with
the figure of Ereshkigal. The limbic brain, with the prefontal

neocortex processes, functions to preserve the species: nurturance, empathy, social bonding. These are roughly analogous to behaviors associated with Inanna.

86. Penelope Shuttle and Peter Redgrove, *The Wise Wound: Eve's Curse and Everywoman.*

87. Karen Elias-Button, "The Dark Mother in Contemporary Women's Poetry," in *Anima, An Experiential Journal,* vol. 4, no. 2, p. 8.

88. Rich, *Poems,* p. 193.

89. The major difference in masculine development is that until recently—and then often only in the second half of life—most men have not needed to go down into the repressed depths once they have initially freed themselves from their childhood and identified with the ideals of the culture, for they have been supported by the outside world without inner dissonance. Increasingly, as there is no adequate masculine wholeness pattern that is collectively sanctioned to form a model of masculine ego development, and as the heroic ego ideal is also found inadequate, more and more are men forced to relate differently to their own depths, and to dare the individual descents that permit them to reclaim repressed instinct and image patterns.

90. Heidel, pp. 122-123.

91. Kramer, *Sacred Marriage Rite,* p. 113.

92. Jacobsen, p. 95.

93. Ibid., p. 110.

94. The god An intimates that the bull on earth will cause seven years of famine (Heidel, p. 53). Ishtar and her votaries mourn its death when Gilgamesh and Enkidu, claiming their mortal power against nature's, slay it (ibid., p. 54).

95. Jacobsen, p. 98.

96. Ibid., p. 99.

97. Kerényi, "Kore," in Jung and Kerényi, *Science of Mythology,* p. 139.

98. Kramer, *Sacred Marriage Rite,* p. 114.

99. Mircea Eliade, "Terra Mater and Cosmic Hierogamies," in *Spring 1955,* p. 35.

100. Ibid., p. 38.

101. Ibid., p. 39.

102. Neumann, *Great Mother,* pp. 192-194.

103. Eliade, "Terra Mater," p. 39.

104. This may be analogous to the demon-ridden emergence of Inanna, born again from the underworld (see below, chap. 9).

105. Kramer, *Sacred Marriage Rite*, pp. 69-70. It might be argued, according to "orthodox" Jungian theory, that this acceptance of the brother instead of the father is a good one. But this may be deceptive. The brother animus may also take a woman from her own necessity or serve as a spokesman for the mother's animus (Patricia Finley, personal communication). In Inanna's poems her mother, Ningal, urges the match with Dumuzi. Ningal is said to be a daughter of Enki and thus is given some sisterly kinship with Dumuzi. She and Utu urge Inanna to accept the shepherd as her consort (ibid., p. 76).

106. Jung, "The Dual Mother," in *Collected Works*, vol. 5, pars. 464-612.

107. Jung, *The Visions Seminars*, pp. 118-119.

108. Jung, *Collected Works*, vol. 14, par. 43, n. 66.

109. Ibid., par. 43.

110. Ibid., par. 44, n. 72.

111. To my knowledge, there is no mention in Sumerian-Akkadian material of the awareness of such energy and consciousness centers. But I feel certain from the careful ordering of garments that such an interpretation is not far-fetched. And Joseph Campbell, in a lecture, has suggested that the sevenfold interlacement of the two serpents on the Babylonian Gudea cup (ca. 2000 B.C.) may symbolize the kundalini and its chakras.

112. Neumann, *Great Mother*, p. 160.

113. Ibid. For a description of Egyptian female gate guardians, see *Egyptian Book of the Dead*, chap. 147.

114. See S.P. Mason, *A History of the Sciences*.

115. Apuleius describes his Roman initiation into the mysteries of Isis: "I approach the confines of death. Having trod the threshold of Proserpina, I return through all the elements. At midnight I beheld the sun brightly shining. I was in the presence of the gods above and the gods below."

116. Wolkstein and Kramer.

117. Ibid.

118. Jacobsen, pp. 124-125.

119. The same word is used for all three substances (ibid., p. 111).

120. Elizabeth Williams Forte, *Ancient Near Eastern Seals*, nos. 39, 41.

121. James Hillman writing of Tiresias in *The Myth of Analysis,* p. 280.

122. McKell, pp. 208ff.

123. Jacobsen, p. 111.

124. Red is a color that scholars have associated particularly with Enki in Sumer (Forte, no. 37, n.).

125. Kramer, *Sacred Marriage Rite,* pp. 166-167.

126. Wolkstein and Kramer.

127. Ibid.

128. Edward C. Whitmont, "The Magic Dimension of Consciousness"; and Ujhely.

129. Kramer, *Sacred Marriage Rite,* p. 116.

130. Ibid.

131. One of the problems for the male therapist who is not at home in these deeper layers of the psyche—when feeling enveloped by the feminine and not understanding what level of the feminine—is that he may register the intimacy as sexual, especially when the transference is eroticized in its polymorphism. For a woman, a male therapist's interpretive or physical response (to her need for primal intimacy in an undifferentiated, genital erotic way) can feel like a betrayal. It is not what she needs, although she herself may not know that until later.

132. Jung, *Collected Works,* vol. 9, pt. II, par. 339.

133. Jung, *Visions Seminars,* p. 91.

134. Jung, "The Symbolic Life," in *Collected Works,* vol. 18, par. 631.

135. Wolkstein and Kramer.

136. Neumann says: "Because the feminine has been humiliated and misused as a pleasure object, it avenges itself by regressing to matriarchal hostility toward the male" ("Psychological Stages of Feminine Development," p. 86). His perspective is patriarchal, based on an adversary position only. It barely hints at the larger issues inherent in the return of Inanna and modern women to the dark goddess.

137. Kramer, *Sacred Marriage Rite,* p. 105.

138. Ibid., p. 156, n. 25.

139. Jacobsen, pp. 26-27.

140. Ibid., p. 26.

141. Kramer, *Sacred Marriage Rite,* pp. 81, 59; and Jacobsen, p. 46.

142. Kramer, *Sacred Marriage Rite,* p. 118.

143. Ibid., p. 119.
144. Wolkstein and Kramer.
145. Kramer, *Sacred Marriage Rite,* p. 119.
146. Jacobsen, pp. 49-52.
147. Wolkstein and Kramer.
148. Kramer, *Sacred Marriage Rite,* p. 128.
149. Ibid., pp. 63ff, 92, 100.
150. Ibid., p. 122.
151. Jacobsen, pp. 27-28.
152. Ibid., p. 62.
153. Ibid., p. 27.
154. James Hillman, "On Psychological Femininity," in *Myth of Analysis,* pp. 215-298.

Bibliography

Berry, Patricia. "The Rape of Demeter/Persephone and Neurosis." *Spring 1975.*

Christ, Carol P., and Plaskow, Judith, eds. *Womanspirit Rising, A Feminist Reader in Religion.* San Francisco: Harper & Row, 1979.

De Nicolas, Antonio T. *Meditations through the Rig-Veda: Four-Dimensional Man.* Boulder and London: Shambhala, 1978.

Campbell, Joseph. *Myths to Live By.* New York: Viking Press, 1972.

Dinerstein, Dorothy. *The Mermaid and the Minotaur: Sexual Arrangements and Human Malaise.* New York: Harper & Row, 1977.

Fierz-David, Linda. "Psychological Reflections on the Fresco Series of the Villa of the Mysteries in Pompeii." Mimeographed. Zurich, 1957.

Forte, Elizabeth Williams. *Ancient Near Eastern Seals: A Selection of Stamp and Cylinder Seals from the Collection of Mrs. William H. Moore.* New York: Metropolitan Museum of Art, 1976.

Gebser, Jean. "The Foundations of the Aperspective World." Extracts in *Main Currents of Modern Thought,* vol. 29 (1972) no. 2; vol. 30 (1973), no. 3.

Guntrip, Harry. *Schizoid Phenomena, Object Relations, and the Self.* New York: International Universities Press, 1969.

Harding, M. Esther. *Woman's Mysteries, Ancient and Modern.* New York: Harper & Row, 1976.

Harrison, Jane Ellen. *Prolegomena to the Study of Greek Religion.* Cambridge: Cambridge University Press, 1922.

Heidel, Alexander. *The Gilgamesh Epic and Old Testament Parallels.* Chicago: University of Chicago Press, 1946.

Heilbrun, Carolyn G. *Reinventing Womanhood.* New York: W.W. Norton & Co., 1979.

Hillman, James. *The Myth of Analysis: Three Essays in Archetypal Psychology.* Evanston: Northwestern University Press, 1972.

Jacobsen, Thorkild. *The Treasures of Darkness: A History of Mesopotamian Religion.* New Haven: Yale University Press, 1976.

Jung, C.G. *The Collected Works* (Bollingen Series XX). 20 vols., trans. R.F.C. Hull, ed. H. Read, M. Fordham, G. Adler, Wm. McGuire. Princeton: Princeton University Press, 1953-1979.

――――. *The Visions Seminars* (1930-34). 2 vols. Zurich: Spring Publications, 1976.

――――, and Kerényi, C. *Essays on a Science of Mythology: The Myth of the Divine Child and the Mysteries of Eleusis.* New York: Harper & Row, 1949.

Kerényi, Karl. *Athene, Virgin and Mother.* Zurich: Spring Publications, 1978.

Kingsley, David R. *The Sword and the Flute: Kali and Krsna, Dark Visions of the Terrible and the Sublime in Hindu Mythology.* Berkeley: University of California Press, 1975.

Kohut, Heinz. *The Analysis of Self.* New York: International Universities Press, 1971.

Kramer, Samuel Noah. *From the Poetry of Sumer: Creation, Glorification, Adoration.* Berkeley: University of California Press, 1979.

――――. *The Sacred Marriage Rite: Aspects of Faith, Myth, and Ritual in Ancient Sumer.* Bloomington: Indiana University Press, 1969.

――――. *Sumerian Mythology: A Study of Spiritual and Literary Achievement in the Third Millenium B.C.* New York: Harper & Row, 1961.

Mason, S.P. *A History of the Sciences.* New York: Collier, rev. ed., 1962.

Massell, Sylvia Perera. "The Scapegoat Complex." *Quadrant,* vol. 12 (1979), no. 2.

Masson, Margaret W. "The Typology of the Female as a Model for the Regenerate: Puritan Preaching, 1690-1730." *Signs, Journal of Women in Culture and Society,* vol. 2 (1976), no. 2.

McKell, Kimberley. *The Psychology of the Tantric Chakras.* University Microfilms International, 1978.

Neumann, Erich. *The Great Mother: An Analysis of the Archetype.* Princeton: Princeton University Press, 1955.

――――. "On the Moon and Matriarchal Consciousness." *Fathers and*

Mothers: Five Papers on the Archetypal Background of Family Psychology. Zurich: Spring Publications, 1973.

———. *The Origins and History of Consciousness.* Princeton: Princeton University Press, 1970.

———. "Psychological Stages of Feminine Development." *Spring 1959.*

Olsen, Tillie. *Silences.* New York: Delta/Seymour Lawrence, 1979.

Rama, Swami; Ballentine, Rudolph; and Ajaya, Swami. *Yoga and Psychotherapy: The Evolution of Consciousness.* Honesdale, Pa.: The Himalayan Institute, 1976.

Rich, Adrienne. *On Lies, Secrets, and Silences: Selected Prose, 1966-1978.* New York: W.W. Norton & Co., 1979.

———. *Poems: Selected and New, 1950-1974.* New York: W.W. Norton & Co., 1974.

———. *Of Woman Born: Motherhood as Experience and Institution.* New York: W.W. Norton & Co., 1976.

Rosaldo, Michelle Zimbalist, and Lamphere, Louise, eds. *Woman, Culture, and Society.* Stanford: Stanford University Press, 1974.

Shuttle, Penelope, and Redgrove, Peter. *The Wise Wound: Eve's Curse and Everywoman.* New York: Richard Marek Publishers,1978.

Ujhely, Gertrude. "Thoughts Concerning the *Causa Finalis* of the Cognitive Mode Inherent in Pre-Oedipal Psychopathology." Diploma Thesis. C.G. Jung Training Center. New York, 1980.

Von Franz, Marie-Louise. *Problems of the Feminine in Fairytales.* Zurich: Spring Publications, 1972.

———. *The Psychological Meaning of Redemption Motifs in Fairytales.* Toronto: Inner City Books, 1980.

———. *Shadow and Evil in Fairytales.* Zurich: Spring Publications,1974.

Washbourne, Penelope, ed. *Seasons of Woman: Song, Poetry, Ritual, Prayer, Myth, Story.* San Francisco: Harper & Row, 1979.

Whitmont, Edward C. "The Magic Dimension of Consciousness." *Spring 1956.*

———. "The Momentum of Man: The Cultural Evolution of the Masculine and Feminine." *Quadrant,* vol. 9 (1976), no. 1.

Wolkstein, Diane, and Kramer, Samuel Noah. *Inanna, Queen of Heaven and Earth: Her Stories and Hymns.* Forthcoming.

Woodman, Marion. *The Owl Was a Baker's Daughter: Obesity, Anorexia Nervosa, and the Repressed Feminine.* Toronto: Inner City Books, 1980.

Zabriskie, Beverley. "Isis, Ancient Goddess, Modern Woman." Diploma Thesis. C.G. Jung Training Center, New York, 1980.

Index

Studies in Jungian Psychology
by Jungian Analysts

Sewn Paperbacks

New, recent and choice:

The Scapegoat Complex: Toward a Mythology of Shadow and Guilt.
Sylvia Brinton Perera (New York). ISBN 0-919123-22-8. 128 pp. $14

Addiction to Perfection: The Still Unravished Bride.
Marion Woodman (Toronto). ISBN 0-919123-11-2. Illustrated. 208 pp. $17

The Creation of Consciousness: Jung's Myth for Modern Man.
Edward F. Edinger, M.D. (Los Angeles). ISBN 0-919123-13-9. Illustrated. 128 pp. $14

The Illness That We Are: A Jungian Critique of Christianity.
John P. Dourley (Ottawa). ISBN 0-919123-16-3. 128 pp. $14

Alchemy: An Introduction to the Symbolism and the Psychology.
Marie-Louise von Franz (Zurich). ISBN 0-919123-04-X. 84 illustrations. 288 pp. $18

The Pregnant Virgin: A Process of Psychological Transformation.
Marion Woodman (Toronto). ISBN 0-919123-20-1. Illustrated. 208 pp. $17

The Jungian Experience: Analysis and Individuation.
James A. Hall, M.D. (Dallas). ISBN 0-919123-25-2. 176 pp. $16

Phallos: Sacred Image of the Masculine.
Eugene Monick (Scranton/New York). ISBN 0-919123-26-0. 30 illustrations. 144 pp. $15

The Christian Archetype: A Jungian Commentary on the Life of Christ.
Edward F. Edinger, M.D. (Los Angeles). ISBN 0-919123-27-9. Illustrated. 144 pp. $15

Personality Types: Jung's Model of Typology.
Daryl Sharp (Toronto). ISBN 0-919123-30-9. Diagrams. 128 pp. $14

The Psychological Meaning of Redemption Motifs in Fairytales.
Marie-Louise von Franz (Zurich). ISBN 0-919123-01-5. 128 pp. $14

The Sacred Prostitute: Eternal Aspect of the Feminine.
Nancy Qualls-Corbett (Birmingham). ISBN 0-919123-31-7. Illustrated. 176 pp. $16

The Survival Papers: Anatomy of a Midlife Crisis.
Daryl Sharp (Toronto). ISBN 0-919123-34-1. 160 pp. $15

The Cassandra Complex: Living with Disbelief.
Laurie Layton Schapira (New York). ISBN 0-919123-35-X. Illustrated. 160 pp. $15

The Ravaged Bridegroom: Masculinity in Women.
Marion Woodman (Toronto). ISBN 0-919123-42-2. Illustrated. 224 pp. $18

Liberating the Heart: Spirituality and Jungian Psychology.
Lawrence W. Jaffe (Los Angeles). ISBN 0-919123-43-0. 176 pp. $16

The Dream Story.
Donald Broadribb (W. Australia). ISBN 0-919123-45-7. 256pp. $18

The Rainbow Serpent: Bridge to Consciousness.
Robert L. Gardner (Toronto). ISBN 0-919123-46-5. Illustrated. 128 pp. $15

Circle of Care: Clinical Issues in Jungian Psychology.
Warren Steinberg (New York). ISBN 0-919123-47-3. 160 pp. $16

Jung Lexicon: A Primer of Terms & Concepts.
Daryl Sharp (Toronto). ISBN 0-919123-48-1. Diagrams. 160 pp. $16

Prices and payment (check or money order) in $U.S. (in Canada, $Cdn)
Add Postage/Handling: 1-2 books, $2; 3-4 books, $4; 5-8 books, $7
Write for complete free Catalogue

INNER CITY BOOKS
Box 1271, Station Q, Toronto, Canada M4T 2P4